MW00529543

"With compassion, wit, and piercing honesty, Emily Mester delves into our love of consumerism—and what our desires say about who we want to become. Bravely personal, incisively critical, *American Bulk* is a report on our national psyche and a captivating family story."

—Larissa Pham, author of National Book Critics Circle John Leonard finalist *Pop Song*

"A funny, incisive, humane dispatch from a brilliant new voice in nonfiction. *American Bulk* had me cringing, laughing, and yes, even tearing up as it drew the contours of my own, and our national, appetites. I remain amazed that a book so clear-eyed in its scrutiny of our capitalistic perversity left me with so much hope."

—Melissa Febos, author of *Girlhood*, winner of the National Book Critics Circle Award in Criticism

"*American Bulk* is composed of some of my favorite nonfiction essays on family, capital, love, and dysfunction that I've ever read. It's a refreshing and needed reframing of what all these things mean, today, right now, as the neon haze of fast-food signs flicker from their longtime dominion of the American experience. Emily Mester examines our compulsion to consume with careful incisions that I kept highlighting and coming back to, just to whisper the words to myself to make their clear-eyed cleverness my own."

—Arabelle Sicardi, author of *The House of Beauty* (forthcoming)

American Bulk

Essays on Excess

Emily Mester

W. W. NORTON & COMPANY

Independent Publishers Since 1923

For information about permission to reproduce selections from this book,
write to Permissions, W. W. Norton & Company, Inc., 500 Fifth Avenue,
New York, NY 10110

For information about special discounts for bulk purchases, please contact
W. W. Norton Special Sales at specialsales@wwnorton.com or 800-233-4830

Manufacturing by Lakeside Book Company
Production manager: Delaney Adams

ISBN 978-1-324-03523-7 (pbk)

W. W. Norton & Company, Inc.
500 Fifth Avenue, New York, NY 10110
www.wwnorton.com

W. W. Norton & Company Ltd.
15 Carlisle Street, London W1D 3BS

10 9 8 7 6 5 4 3 2 1

HB 08 03 2024 0709

I need a truck to haul my pain
I need a truck just to haul around my name
I need a truck to haul the womens from my bed
I need a truck to haul my body when I'm dead

I need a truck to haul my guns to town
I need a truck to haul my bad thoughts around
I need a truck to haul my Percodan and gin
And I need a truck to haul all my trucks in

    —WARREN ZEVON

Contents

Introduction

A FIFTY-FOOT SPIKE ON WHICH entire cars are speared like kebabs rises from the asphalt in the Cermak Plaza parking lot. I ask my grandma how many people died to make it, but she says nobody, it's just art. She asks me if I can count the cars for her, so I squeeze one eye shut and make dots with my finger on the fogged car window; there's eight. Woolly heat is blasting from the vents and in our puffy coats we fill the whole back seat of the minivan. My brothers and my parents are in the Service Merchandise with all the glass cases, buying another clock radio.

Every Sunday we do this. We go to our favorite stores. The trick to getting something is to ask Dad when his cart is full and he's close to the registers, when he seems happy and light. My mom will say I don't need it, so I don't ask her, but Dad will say *Sure* and she'll sigh and I'll add to his pile. The piles in carts become piles in bags. On the way out of the store he'll put his hand around the back of my neck and squeeze it hard, and if I don't squirm away he'll say *She's tough* in a proud voice. When we bring all the bags into the house, they'll sit there full for days, sometimes weeks. Then he'll empty the bags and put the piles on the dining room table, which is for eating only on Thanksgiving and Christmas. Every other day, it's for piles.

Sometimes I choose a toy or a book, but some stores force you to be creative, like the Sports Authority, where I scoured the store for something to want and finally came upon a row of glittering plastic fish. All the stores have candy, but my parents don't always let me get candy. I grabbed a Kit Kat once and hid it under my shirt, and nobody saw so I did it again at REI, and then at Lowe's, but then my brothers caught me. Dad said I couldn't leave my room for a week and could have only bread and water because that's what it was like in prison, but on the first night my mom let me sneak downstairs and gave me cheese on saltines and by the second night the punishment was over.

Sometimes you try your hardest and still can't find something to want. The dark lizard store where my brothers buy fish food is like that. Radio Shack is like that. Home Depot is like that, just knobs and wood. You can't even pee in the toilets, they have plastic over them. Service Merchandise is a showroom, which my mom says is why they don't let you grab anything off the shelves. Instead, you have to take a little paper ticket to a man at a window and he gets things for you. This doesn't interest me, so I stay in the car with Grandma. The sky and the parking lot are the same color and everybody walks fast to their cars with their breath in front of them. My grandma says she's starting to sweat so I roll the window down a little. The sliver of cold makes the warm car even cozier. It smells like Christmas because of the evergreens they sell across the street, and McDonald's because of the McDonald's. The toy right now is Cabbage Patch Kids if you say girl. A Tonka truck if you say boy.

My brain has words and colors and shapes and if I can match them up, my grandma says *Wow honey*. Once, I told her the longest word I knew: Slow-buh-dom Muh-loh-suh-vitch, and she was so impressed she had me say it again for my parents, and then my parents' friends, and now I say it unprompted when I want to show an adult that I'm aware of the things they are aware of. I don't know who he is, just that he's in the news. The brightest things I can see out the car window are the store signs, which match the ones you see on TV. If the letters on the screen are looped and red, a woman will say *Walgreens*. If the letters are white and tilting, a man will say *Circuit City*.

My grandma teaches reading in Iowa, but I'm only three or four so nobody has asked me to read yet. I squint through the window at the loopy red letters across the parking lot and say what I've heard the woman on TV say. I say *Walgreens*. My grandma asks me to do it again. I say it again the way I say Slow-buh-dom Muh-loh-suh-vitch, stretching it out. With awe, she declares that I'm reading. But I'm not reading. I don't know which letters go with which sounds yet. I just know which TV sound goes with each picture. My parents and brothers get back in the car and my grandma shares the news. I don't remember their pride, but I do remember hers. For decades, she will return to it. *You read without instruction, I always knew you were special.* Without instruction means nobody taught you how. But what are advertisements if not instructions? For how to find the Walgreens in any parking lot, any strip mall, any lifetime? Reading means you look at letters and know not only what they say but what they mean. And once you know what they mean you can feel things about them. So I guess I was reading. I saw Walgreens and the TV voice in my head said *Walgreens* and then it was all in me, the frictionless glide of the automatic doors, the glowing rows of Gatorade reflected in the convex security mirrors, the mechanized purr of a complimentary blood-pressure kiosk squeezing me tighter and tighter while my mom waited for medicines. I thought it was a test to see how much squeezing you could tolerate. Walgreens wasn't like school or home. You came in with a list of everything you needed and left with the list crossed off. Handing the money and getting the thing and crossing it off was so much neater a pleasure than the doing, like the click of a lid, or a beep. The doing was not a click. There were so many ways to get caught in the doing. After the pleasure of crossing off *toilet bowl cleaner* came the cleaning of the toilet bowl. But what if you never left? You could have only clicks and beeps, getting and never having to do. I would've lived there if I could, inside the getting, inside the cuff, inside the store, a child in a warm car that never left the parking lot.

American Bulk

Storm Lake, Part 1

WHEN SHE EATS FAST FOOD, before she throws her trash away, she crumples up each piece and stuffs it into some container, a soda cup or a burger box, trash squeezed into trash, because she says it's better for the landfills. Whenever she gets on a plane, she gets off having made friends with her seatmate and will tell you their story all the way to baggage claim. When she walks into a restaurant with a mirrored wall she says *Look, that's a trick to make the place seem bigger.* When she eats fruit she eats everything, even the rind.

My grandma loves anything she can get for free. When I was a kid, she taught me the meaning of the word *complimentary*, and together we scoured restaurants and supermarkets, doctors' offices and bulletin boards, bank counters, information booths, libraries, looking for anything we were allowed to take. We collected papers: business cards, pamphlets, paint samples at Home Depot, cardboard fans to cool us in the summer heat courtesy of our local bank. Once, on a visit to Orlando, in the foyer of a Ruby Tuesday, we hit the jackpot: a wooden kiosk as tall as me and filled with dozens of brochures for tourist attractions, a small sign encouraging us to *Take one: they're free!* We loaded our fanny packs with glossy ads for princess brunches and booze cruises. Here was an Atlantis of freebies thriving just beneath the consumer landscape, and we had discovered it. We learned what bounties could be had for nothing. We redrew the line between trash and everything else.

I was in love with her. If the rest of my family was tense and beady, bad at hugging, irritated in crowds, then my grandma was like a civilian Santa Claus, jolly, ample, white-haired with open arms in an oversize sweatshirt. She told good stories, loved Arby's as much as I did, and was the only person I'd ever met who earnestly said *shucks*. We were scared of the same things—murderers, primarily—and watched *Dateline* together to thrill with fear. She loved celebrities and their gossip; she loved Will Smith and Engelbert Humperdinck and the Royal Family and Rosie O'Donnell. Her pockets were filled with napkins she'd use to wipe sweat off her face and she knew everything there was to know about JonBenét Ramsey. She pronounced Dior like *dyer*, liked to use the word *facetious*, called me a ham. Told me she wanted her gravestone to say *I Told You I Was Sick*. She carried the unmistakable glow of an adored teacher. Whenever she came to our house, Grandma would bring me gifts, plastic bags full of bright, small things, little toys from the dollar store and lipstick samples from the Avon lady and stacks of thin paperbacks. When I was seven, we finally decided to take a trip to the town in western Iowa where my grandma lived. I wanted to see everything: the classroom she taught in, her neighbors, her favorite gas station, the grocery store, and of course, her house. I imagined her house like these big bags, brimming and piled with affection.

Before she retired and moved to Illinois, my grandma lived in her Storm Lake house for thirty-six years. For the last twelve years, after her husband died suddenly, she lived in it alone. When I was a kid, she would come to visit us in Illinois a few times a year, and I was always the person most excited to see her. But we almost never came to see her in Iowa. Her life outside us was a mystery to me. She wove me a vast and familiar repertoire of tales from the place. Some were charming, like the tailor who thought her father's slacks were for a child, or the town drunk walking into the wrong house. She talked about the farm and the rolltop desk she loved as a child, the way my dad would hide his vitamins behind the microwave and hoard peaches in his cheeks. A few of her stories were sad, like the ones about her student JD, so poor his family ate ketchup sandwiches, whose funeral announcement mentioned his love of "pokeymon," who said one day *I might as well go get hit by a car*, and then did. But Storm Lake never felt dark, or desolate. It fascinated me.

The drive from the Chicago suburbs was seven hours long, and when we got to Storm Lake, we immediately went to fetch Grandma, pulling up to the curb near her house. As I sat in the idling car, I watched my dad walk up and ring her doorbell. I watched the door swing open just wide enough to let her slip out, two plastic bags in hand. She closed and locked it behind her. When she got into the car, I shook with excitement in the seat. *Grandma!* I screamed, *Let's go in!* But she shook her head. *Honey*, she said. *You don't want to see that boring thing*. But I did. It was all I wanted to see. I asked again a few hours later, kept asking throughout the duration of the trip, at the family farm, as she watched me swim in the little hotel pool, at a restaurant called G Witters where I ordered a BLT without the L and the T, and each time, she refused. Later, my parents told me that she wouldn't let us see it because it was messy. They used the word *embarrassed*.

I had seen this ritual before. The adults around me loved to apologize for their messes, tossing *I'm sorry* around without thinking, like *please* and *thank you*. I heard it from my best friend's parents when my mom came to pick me up. I heard it from my first-grade teacher when we rode in her car on a field trip, and I heard it from my mom, sometimes, to people who couldn't possibly care, like the plumber or the exterminator. Everyone seemed *embarrassed* by the way they lived, but their shame was usually directed outward. I'd never seen an embarrassment thick enough to keep out family.

Whenever she and I set foot in a hotel, our little brains burst into flame. We learned that not only could you get a new set of soaps each day to take home, but also the slippers, the embossed pen and notepad on the desk, the little packets of instant coffee, front-desk mints, and even the hidden freebies most guests didn't think to take: the spare roll of toilet paper, the Kleenex, and sometimes, if you stumbled into luck, an extra shampoo stolen from the maid's unattended supply cart. At the post office there were free Tyvek mailers. At McDonald's, ketchup and salt packets, straws, and napkins by the fistful. And later, from the internet, promotional materials that arrived by mail. Once, in grade school, I sent away for free swag promoting sudden infant death syndrome awareness. It was summer when the box finally came. My cousin was visiting, and I eagerly showed her my haul: they had sent me not just literature but also magnets, pins, bookmarks, a full-size poster, all emblazoned with a ribbon of pink and blue. *They'll send you tons of stuff*, I explained to her coolly. *You just have to say you're a doctor.*

It had not seemed like a big deal. I thought of all the stuff my psychiatrist mom got free from pharmaceutical companies, the Xanax highlighters, the gel-grip Depakote pens, lavished on her in the hope that day after day she'd see the free pen, and day after day think nothing of it, until one day, at the end of some appointment, with the pen poised above the prescription pad, she might hear her subconscious whisper to her hand and find herself writing down *Lexapro, 20 mg*. For my mom to accept the pen required no promise, and that was the beauty of free stuff. It wasn't transactional; it was more like a wish.

But my cousin scolded me. It was wrong to lie in order to get things, and doubly wrong if you got things for which you had no use. *It's wasteful*, she said, and so I stood with her in a park and gave it all away, wincing each time I handed a SIDS brochure to another confused stranger. The first part of my cousin's argument made sense, but the second one was lost on me. How could I waste the pamphlets just by having them? Wasting something meant the opposite of having it, like when I didn't finish my food at a restaurant and my grandma would offer to eat what remained, no matter how mangled or meager it was. After the meal, as the rest of the family zipped up their coats, I'd stand next to her and watch her inspect the floor, the table, and the crevices in the booth to make sure we hadn't left anything behind. Sometimes she'd notice a pen or a fallen mitten. Otherwise, after a few moments, I'd gently say

Grandma, nothing's there, and she'd reluctantly follow me to the
door, stealing glances back at the table until she couldn't anymore. Where my cousin saw waste as a form of excess—it was
having something you didn't need—my grandma saw waste as
the act of a careless and unimaginative person. It was looking at
what could easily be yours, and assuming that you'd never need
it. A type of rejection. To leave the spear of pickle, or the tough,
curly piece of kale on which your appetizer sat, to ignore the
decorative umbrella in your drink, the packet of crayons with
your kids' menu, the penny on the floor, to let something go
to the trash when it could go in your belly, your pocket, your
purse—that was a waste.

My parents didn't understand my grandma's obsession with
free and cheap stuff either. My dad, especially, was irritated by
his mother's habits. On family trips, he'd cast an eye at her lug-
gage as we checked out of the hotel, asking her if she took the
shower curtains, too. Once, we took a family trip to Japan and,
upon landing back at O'Hare, were detained for half an hour at
customs because they'd found something suspicious in her bag.
We watched as the border agent carefully unzipped the suitcase
and began to empty its contents. His sternness softened into
confusion. The bag was large, but contained only a few pairs
of slacks, T-shirts, some prescription bottles, all of which were
swallowed by a messy pile of all the souvenirs my grandma
had collected throughout the journey. Out of the bag he lifted
crumpled napkins, coffee filters, two weeks' worth of mini-
shampoos, and finally, the offending item: an ordinary apple
she'd saved from the hotel breakfast, tossed in with the rest of
her things and carried across six thousand miles of ocean. My

dad rolled his eyes and mumbled *Just packing the essentials*. His suitcases were expertly packed and were, along with his walking shoes, his utility vest, his camera case, and his camera, all purchased especially for this trip. My mom sighed. The agent frowned and threw the fruit in the garbage.

My mom had a reason to be baffled; she's never cared much about collecting things, free or otherwise. Once a year, she'll spend $200 at Ann Taylor Loft, or buy a purse at the outlet mall, and this is as close as she gets to extravagance. But my dad is just as obsessed with acquiring stuff as his mother; the only difference is that she is very cheap, and he very spendy. When I was younger, she spreed in handouts and dollar-store finds, and he at Dick's Sporting Goods and the hardware section of Sears. My grandma thought my dad wasted his money, and he thought she wasted her time. They chalked their fighting up to fundamental differences: she was frugal, he was ravenous.

In Dante's *Inferno*, the tightfisted misers and the extravagant spenders meet in the circle of hell called Greed, where they charge at each other with heavy boulders until the stones crash together. *Why castest thou away?* asks the miser to the spender. *Why holdest thou so fast?* he hears in response. *Inferno*'s moral compass is bland and dubious; it's a glorified cop show that we call high art. I don't know if I see either of these types as sinners, but there is a fundamental truth in the way they interact. They think that they clash because they're opposites. But the impulses that drive them are exactly the same.

Grandma retired a couple years after we visited her in Storm Lake. On her last day, the teachers at Truesdale Elementary School threw her a party. She had been beloved by four decades' worth of students. I remember a fifth grader, Ross, who loved horses and would draw her pictures of the ones he one day wanted to ride. On one visit, she brought a picture he'd done just for me. Her friends, her students, her colleagues—everyone asked her why she couldn't stay longer. Maybe she asked herself that, too. She'd never been proud to be a mother, and certainly never a wife, but she'd always been proud of her teaching. She was good at it, a fact that not even my dad—who took to mocking Iowans the moment he stopped being one—could deny. But despite their differences, my dad wanted her to live nearby, and she wanted to be near her grandchildren, and anyway Storm Lake, she felt, wasn't the same anymore. The people she knew were leaving in droves or else dying, and so within weeks she was on a plane to Chicago, having drawn the curtains and locked up the house, having asked her neighbor Bob to keep an eye on it, having left everything behind except those big suitcases, having left, whether knowing it or not, for good. It was the only time I'd ever seen her pack light.

She came to stay with us for the summer, sleeping on the pullout couch in our basement. I spent hours down there, sitting and chatting, eleven years old now and delighted to have her so close. She told me, with frankness, about her mental health in the wake of retirement, padding around in a Mickey Mouse sleep shirt or her comfy Dockers (*men's clothes just fit better*). *My depression*, she'd call it, pronouncing the first syllable *dee*, instead of *duh*, which made it sound a bit grand. She told me how much she missed Storm Lake, but also how nice it was to be gone. *I've been friendly all my life*, she said wistfully. *But now, I'm excited to be unknown*. She bought a condo in a suburb nearby, nice and empty, and this one, for a while anyway, she allowed me to step inside. Once, and only once, she even let me stay the night. After she said goodnight, my sleeping bag and I were the only things in her new spare bedroom, and I lay with my eyes open, too excited to shut them. As long as the house stayed empty, we could do this whenever we wanted. As long as the house stayed empty, we had nothing but time to fill.

Wholesale

To walk around Costco as a childless, unattached person is to experience the fragility of your existence. To perk up at the reasonably priced Angus steaks only to realize they are not sold in quantities fewer than eight and think, *Well, I guess if I ate one steak a day for a week plus an extra on Sunday*, is to realize the promise of decay. Costco is a place for families, or else individuals of family-size needs: restauranteurs, corporate-picnic planners, fraternity brothers, older couples who eat the same five foods with pious regularity, the clinically depressed who subsist on bulk bags of pretzels and Craisins and little else. It is for ambitious appetites and pathological fears. It is for a scarcity that is anticipated but never realized. The Costco I know, my Costco, is for families.

I have known Costco longer than I have known most of my friends. I have spent more hours roaming its aisles than I have spent with several of my first cousins. My family took our first Costco trip in November 1998. The company had brought a store to the suburbs of Chicago, and we went on the very first Sunday of its opening. I was eight, and every single week for the next six years, my mother, my father, my grandma, my three brothers, and later, when she was born, my sister, would pile into our red minivan and later, a brown SUV, and we would return to that Costco, always that Costco, always together, and always on Sunday. We were nominally Catholic, but nobody ever went to church. Costco was our mass.

Though Costco is for families, not all families can feasibly shop there. The household income of the average Costco shopper is about 50 percent higher than that of the Walmart shopper, while the lower-income shoppers who could most benefit from the savings of buying in bulk are, by and large, priced out of the game, because the ability to shop at Costco and its ilk carries many hidden requirements: membership fees, a car, proximity to a limited set of stores, and of course, more cash up front to buy a pack of eight sirloins in one go instead of just two. Paying less in this way is, ironically, the privilege of the relatively comfortable.

But Costco doesn't seem upscale. In the hierarchy of retail aesthetics, Costco sits at the unsexy bottom. It lacks the earthy bourgeois glamour of Whole Foods, or Target's warm graphic buoyancy, or the hot American urgency of 7-Eleven. Even the average supermarket shelf stimulates, an eye-pleasing array organized carefully by color, flavor, and brand. By contrast, a Costco store carries all the visual allure of a warehouse. Everything within its walls is large, limited, and random. Where your average grocery store carries about forty thousand different products, Costco carries a tenth of that amount. There are two types of mayonnaise and they both come in tubs. You can buy an eighteen-piece artisan spice rack, but not a jar of oregano. Even the fourteen-year aged cheddar comes in huge blocks whose size-to-price ratio seems to throw the cheese's rarity into doubt. Where a supermarket greets you with bursting crates of produce, inclined at an angle toward the shopper as if to say *Welcome*, Costco's produce, though equally fresh, sits at the back of the store in a frigid locker, prepackaged in plastic sleeves and cardboard boxes, unsqueezable.

In other words, Costco is quality without the usual trimmings of quality. Even the luxury goods seem utilitarian, leached of their sheen. Spanish saffron is the costliest spice in the world, and the finest variety comes from the Castilla–La Mancha region, where the flower blooms and dies in a single November day, its delicate red spindles harvested by hand. Costco is the world's largest importer of genuine La Mancha saffron, and in the warehouse, you'll find it under pallets of tube socks, in blister packaging, the words KIRKLAND SIGNATURE emblazoned across the front. Their affordable vodka is rumored to be made at the same French distillery as Grey Goose, but by now you can guess whose bottle features a magnificent glacial landscape dotted by white wings, and whose simply says, in block text, VODKA.

———

Costco is attractive to the rich and the comfortable, then, but its thrill does not lie in its beauty or prestige, nor even in its savings. Spending fifty cents less per roll of toilet paper is not something that will impact most Costcoans' quality of life. It's also just a clunky way to get groceries; there are many things that the store does not sell, or does not sell in practical quantities. Though my family went to Costco every week, my mom still bought most of our food at the supermarket.

What joy, then, does Costco offer? What dream is born of balsamic vinegar in liters, spices by the pound, and rafts of maxi pads? Costco is not for what you need. It's for what you want.

My dad loves to shop. Compulsively, in fact, and across all consumer categories. Where some spending addicts pour money into a few special interests, say shoes, or books, my dad throws it everywhere, all the time. He walks the aisles of Costco not with a list of things he needs, but with the wide eyes of a child in a toy store. He fills the cart with cereal and bagels, yes, but also with wrench sets, hole punchers, colorful plastic drinking tumblers, Kirkland brand khaki pants, over and over and despite my mom's protests. And while my dad might not spend like the average Costco shopper, his neuroses are its collective, beating heart. It's true that Costco gets you more for your money, but it seems like the discount is only a secondary pleasure. It's not the money part that inspires a cultlike devotion. It's the *more*. Spend time in any Costco, and you'll feel it too. The joy of Costco does not lie in thrift. It lies in bulk.

My dad loves to say *fuck 'em*. I wonder if he said it at his fancy East Coast university, humming it as he served his rich classmates meatloaf in the dining hall, turning it over with his tongue like a worry bead: *fuck 'em, fuck 'em, fuck 'em all*.

His family wouldn't help him pay for college, and when he lost his loans and was kicked out for a semester, he had to return to Iowa to save up. But even with so little money, he still racked up credit card debt buying the kinds of things only a college student would think essential—cotton candy makers, pizza ovens, tieless shoelaces. A rich man now, he buys on a larger scale, but the spirit is the same. He hasn't developed a taste for the finer things. He likes the things he likes.

Far from a harmless quirk, his shopping is a compulsion that has come to define our lives. Every house he's owned he's filled to the brim. The dining rooms are unusable, stacked with new things never opened: Bluetooth headsets, bungee cords, books about weight lifting and the life of Ronald Reagan, bikes, car chargers, suitcases, modular shelves, caffeinated mints, caffeinated soap, digital cameras, microfiber cloths, and DVDs of popular films, even though he only ever watches the same five movies, all of which are either military dramas or buddy comedies, most of which feature a man either killing himself or shitting himself, none of which are *Chocolat*, yet he's got two copies. Offices and family rooms become haphazard storage spaces. The floor of his "shop" is blanketed with tools and nails. The garage is unnavigable, and certainly has never held an actual car. Once every few months, when we were kids, he'd make us clear the rooms out and relocate all the stuff, but they would always fill back up again. If anyone urged him to curb his habit, he would wave them off. *It's my money.*

To people like my dad, Costco offers far more than a good deal. It offers the lulling comfort of permanent volume, the same bulwark against scarcity that draws us to the all-you-can-eat, the BOGO, the unlimited refill, the family size. The endless, the bottomless, the lifetime guarantee—these promises are not to be underestimated, because their flipside is terrifying. To want a boundless supply means also to acknowledge a boundless need. We are inclined to hunger.

Costco keeps its promise of abundance as well as any store can, and for that, most of its customers are loyal for life. I remember, walking through the aisles one Sunday, a long row of displays showing the services one could take advantage of through Costco. Costco could retile your kitchen, change your tires, refinance your home, arrange your Disney vacation, fill your prescriptions, check your eyes, provide your health insurance, build your backyard gazebo, and—my family paused here, stunned for a moment, before an awning labeled *Universal Casket*. Costco had begun to sell coffins, and this was the closest I had ever been to one. I touched the gleaming veneer. Each model had a name. *The Mother. The Kentucky Rose. The Dayton. The Edward. The Lady of Guadalupe.*

Years later, I found the reviews online. All were glowing. *DON'T GET RIPPED OFF IN A TIME OF NEED* warned one; some seemed to speak to the store directly, saying things like *You were there at a time we really needed you, and you didn't let us down*; another reviewer said *I felt my frugal mom would have been very PROUD OF ME*; one wrote ominously *I will purchase again.*

In addition to the hungry and the ill, Costco also appeals to those who fear scarcity in a more literal sense. Their emergency food department is stocked with the dizzying quantities that could only appeal to the truly doom-hearted. For $279.99, you get six hundred servings of canned eggs; $449 gets you twelve cans of freeze-dried ground beef that will last you ninety days. *Unlike fresh meat*, the product copy reads, *THRIVE Ground Beef has a shelf life of 25 years in the can.* For $4,499.99, a single person can gorge for a whole year on a kit of chicken stew, breakfast skillets, and chili mac with beef, all nonperishable. I eventually read those reviews too, some of them from customers who are saving for disaster, others from those for whom the kits comprise their everyday diet.

> If you don't eat them regularly now do not depend on them in an emergency. It takes your body some time to adjust to eating beans, do you really want an upset digestive track during an emergency?
> if mad-money is no problem, or you fear a fruit famine, this product is a real treat
> + Pros:
> easy and tasty
> – Cons:
> none except i sometimes crave a fresh steak

Costco, then, nurses the anxiety of wanting. For those whose greatest fear is empty shelves, it quite literally fills a void. While my mom and siblings were angry and overwhelmed at my dad's buying and at the mess surrounding us, I don't think he ever minded the chaos. Even the most dogged addicts often come to reckon with their habit, to see the damage their high has left in its wake. Not him. He weaves among his piles like a drunk. Serene, moony. When he said *It's my money*, I'd assumed he was asserting his right to spend it. But now, I wonder if he didn't mean it literally. His piles of stuff were the form his money took, the shaky concept of prosperity made flesh. It wasn't enough, for him, to have enough. To be assured of his good fortune, he needed to see it. To pick it up and hold it, as you might a hand.

But for all the absurdity of Costco, all the reasons why our trips there were an unnecessary exercise in privileged accumulation, there is also this: I loved them.

Psychologists like to emphasize the importance of *play*, the activities we do for pleasure and for pleasure's sake alone, the means by which we shape our sense of self. Play is what bonds us. It is imaginative, marked off in some way from reality. It values process over any specific end goal. It is structured, but that structure comes from the shared values of the group. It is, intrinsically, not work. I couldn't imagine my whole family going to the park or the movies together, having game nights, going to school fundraisers. It's not that we never went on other outings, but we were not the kind of group who could comfortably sustain such blatant, undisguised togetherness. We needed a pretext. Costco was our play.

I felt freer there than I did at home. My family was nicer to each other in public, for one. I could also roam throughout the store in ways that most ten-year-olds, in most spaces, cannot. My dad's shopping high made him generous, and he let us buy things my mother never would have, like giant stuffed bears and massive boxes of Fruit Gushers. And I liked the scale of the place, how it was huge but not empty. The windows were few and the ceilings were so high that birds who flew in through the entrance didn't flap around furiously, but instead simply perched there, serene. Costco felt like a fortress in which one could safely hide from anything. As long as I can remember, I have relished that feeling, in school tornado drills and car trips, in snowstorms and sleepovers. For some, the idea of getting locked in a store after closing is a nightmare, but that was my dream, because Costco had everything we'd need. To be warm and full and surrounded was not my idea of being trapped. It was the safest place in the world.

Now that I'm older and live far away, my dad's mess no longer feels like mine. When I return to my parents' house, it's calmer, but I'm always startled by how easily I slip back into the person I was when I left, a sullen teenager. Still, my mom and I have grown closer, begun to confide in each other. After concerted and awkward effort, we have even started saying *I love you* on the phone. I can't say the same of my dad. To talk with him easily, lightly, to chat like friends, feels so unnatural that it makes me physically uncomfortable. I find my voice lowering to a grumble, my words shrinking to monosyllables, my eyes glued to the wall.

If we want to communicate, we need something to pin it on. As a parting gift before I went to graduate school, my parents gave me a small black car. Whenever I visit, Dad spends hours vacuuming the floors and waxing the hood, grumbling that I let it get messy again. He'll email me every so often, asking *How is the Honda?* when he means *How are you?* Occasionally, out of the blue, he'll ask me if I need a new blender or some speaker wire, saying he saw a deal, offering to order it online, and when I say no, I feel real guilt, as if I've rejected a hug. When I first moved into my own apartment, he bought me an EggTastic, one of those As Seen on TV products that sounds far more useful in theory than it is in practice. It's a glorified ceramic mug that lets you make an omelet in the microwave. I pointed out to my dad that cooking an egg is not really a task that requires innovation. But he raved about his EggTastic, and wanted to share with me the gift of convenience. When the package arrived and I stared at the little white-and-yellow cup, the chirpy cartoon lettering, I was struck not by sadness but by the bite of pity that comes when you realize that yes, your parents have always been trying to love you, but trying may not have been enough.

Now that all but one of us has left home, my dad rarely goes to Costco anymore, except for the odd item, or when everyone returns for the holidays and he takes us on what he gleefully calls the Costco Expedition. This isn't to say he's stopped buying. Far from it. If anything, his addiction has ramped up, having shifted mostly to online retail. Packages from Amazon arrive daily. The rise of smartphones and one-click ordering has all but guaranteed that he'll never tire of his hobby, especially given the double high of e-commerce: first when you buy, and again when the package arrives at your door, summoned from great distances by your whims.

When my parents moved to a new house, a big one, their dream home, my mom threatened to leave my dad if he ruined it with stuff. Any purchase he brought into the house would have to be approved by my mother, and she swore not to approve much. We thought that maybe this would end his buying for good, but the house filled anyway. So they bought another one, on a giant patch of farmland, and this began to fill too, but my dad found a solution. The farmland that once held cows could now hold storage sheds. Eventually, he plans to build a warehouse on the property, and it is this, not the beautiful beachfront castle, not the beautiful mountaintop cabin, that I suspect is my dad's dream.

They flew north to help me move in for graduate school. The process involved a trip to Costco; how could it not? The day had been hot and tense. But as we walked into this store, I could sense the tension of the move softening, the screaming over lopsided IKEA shelves more distant, my dad beaming. It had been a while since any of us had been to Costco, and even longer since we'd been there together.

The next day, after my parents left, I found myself sitting on my apartment floor, trying to stain a cheap dresser, tearing up, half with frustration and half with another thing that I couldn't name but felt in my stomach. To say you miss home might indicate you want to return there, and that wasn't quite it. I did not want to go back, and I didn't miss my family's presence so much as I felt their absence. I was pained and made low by the distance of them. Together, we formed an abundance, even if it was a turbulent one. But now, that abundance had been reduced to just me, alone and left to figure out my new life amid a mess of boxes I'd only half unpacked.

But that feeling would come later. In Costco, there were orchids on shelves. Foam pillows. A hot dog that had not changed in price or appearance in over a decade. I know you can't stay anywhere forever. But you can live completely for moments at a time.

Al Forno

ON MY FIRST VISIT TO New York City, I took acid for the first time, in a hotel room with four friends. For most of our visit, we'd been crashing on couches and in childhood bedrooms, but needing the cloistered solitude only a hotel room can afford, we'd booked one for this special night. We scrupulously arranged the room to welcome the toddlers we'd soon become. An array of texturally novel snacks was fanned out on the bedside table: pillowy gummy worms encrusted in sour sugar, crunchy corn puffs that would dissolve into sea-foam in your mouth, Pop Rocks, edible goo. On the desk, music videos played on someone's open laptop, and next to it we laid a stack of blank paper and a set of Magic Markers. The pristine bed was artfully mussed into a nest of blankets and pillows over which we draped ourselves as we waited eagerly for the come-up. For a while, we tried to nudge our mind-doors open by faking the altered state that would soon overtake us for real. *This feels*, I ran my hand along the taupe industrial carpet, crumbs and hair sticking to my palm, *so cool*. Jessy drew the blinds and peered out. *It's weird that I'm in a building*, she said, pausing for dramatic effect. *But I'm also looking at a building.* We nodded with heavy-lidded grins.

An hour or two passed. We colored, snacked. There are two ways to determine for sure whether or not you're on drugs: one, look in a mirror, or two, sit on a toilet. As you stare straight into your reflection or down at your feet, you'll lock eyes with the sober world you inhabited not too long ago and realize, yes, I have been transported. When I peed in the hotel bathroom, though, I realized I was just peeing in a hotel bathroom. My eyes in the mirror met my gaze steadily. The fabric of the world did not shiver. Nothing wobbled at all. *Guys?* I said as I emerged, *I don't feel it.*

Once everyone in the room admitted that the acid we'd been sold—by the friend of a college classmate whom we knew only as White Plains—was definitely not acid, if it was anything at all, we needed another plan. As we stepped out of the lobby, the frigid air sobered us even more. By now, it was eight o'clock. It was too dark and cold to go to a park, too expensive to go to a restaurant, and too late to go to a museum. We were too young for the bars. Someone suggested a church. The right mix of warm, free, and open. I hadn't been to one in years. But when we approached the Church of the Holy Innocents and tugged on the doors, they were locked, quickly disabusing us of the cinematic lie that Catholic churches keep their doors open 24/7 to give solace to those experiencing crises of faith. Walmarts, gas stations, and porn stores do that. Churches close now, just like everything else.

We left the church and began meandering up Seventh Avenue. The clumps of pedestrians began to thicken. I accepted a

brochure from a man on the sidewalk, and the sidewalk wid-
ened. I accepted another brochure. The crowd was so dense
now that it became difficult to walk at a purposeful speed. Then
the sidewalk overtook the street and everything was bathed in
light. The five of us stopped walking and looked around. If you
want to determine for sure that you're not on drugs, the worst
way is to wander into Times Square. Next to me, a seven-foot-
tall Dora the Explorer leaned against a bronze statue that I
thought I recognized as Walt Disney. According to his plaque, he
was a priest. *It's always day here*, I murmured, my face lit up by
the words *YOU ARE HERE*. They were flashing across a red
screen, which zoomed out to show a map of New York City
dotted with Bank of America logos, followed by *SO ARE WE*.
We ducked into the closest warm alcove, and a giant anima-
tronic giraffe welcomed us into the Toys"R"Us. I reached into
my coat pocket and began gnawing on a sour worm.

For the entirety of my weeklong visit, I'd felt thrilled and
out of my depth, clawing through the crowds in a strobing
Brooklyn warehouse or hurrying through a turnstile at Penn
Station. Times Square was said to be a grotesque assault on the
senses, but I'd imagined that assault would be a distillation of
this same urban chaos. Looking at the American Eagle and the
Auntie Anne's, the fluorescent lights and the industrial planters,
the puffy-coated families ambling too slowly through the rab-
ble, I understood now that Times Square wasn't the turbo city.
It was the turbo suburbs. I was in a turbo mall, and for the first
time all week, the sensory assault was a familiar one. Fifteen
minutes north was MoMA, which held fifty billion dollars'
worth of art. Fifteen minutes east was the Chrysler Building, a

gleaming Art Deco ode to the Jazz Age. Here we were in New
York City, the headquarters of wealth and taste, inside Times
Square, the headquarters of something else. Money was here
too, but it was a wholly different kind of money.

———

In the midwestern suburbs, the link between wealth and taste
was hazy. I straightened my hair and contemplated learning
how to skateboard. My closet was filled with JCPenney graphic
T-shirts and shiny Payless sneakers. Wealth was not leveraged
to consume rarer or fancier things than the middle class, but
to consume middle-class things in excess. The aesthetic differences among class strata seemed to be mostly differences of
scale. You bought more stuff at the same shopping mall. You had
three or four cars instead of one or two. You went to Disney and
the Wisconsin Dells every year, not just once, and you went to
chain restaurants every weekend, not just birthdays.

I knew very little about the East Coast besides the fact
that my dad loathed it. My mom's whole family was from Boston, and he felt that they, like all East Coasters, were haughty
about things that were worse. They insisted that a dry Dunkin'
Donuts doughnut hole was better than a hot Krispy Kreme.
They shopped at BJ's when Costco had the deals. They cooed
about rocky capes, reeking harbors, frigid beaches with gritty
gray sand. They got misty-eyed about the American Revolu-
tion but couldn't locate Iowa on a map. They paid great sums
to slurp on oyster guts and had never even had a deep-fried
Oreo. They thought that Boston was basically New York while
Chicago was basically Cleveland. They didn't realize the Great

Lakes had waves; they thought civilization bloomed only near the water.

Before I left for boarding school, I assumed this was the extent of the cultural differences between the Midwest and the East Coast, that whether you aligned with one or the other was a matter of Cubs or Sox, Coke or Pepsi, McDonald's or Burger King. There were no hierarchies to taste, no codes, just a single stream of culture and a game of this or that. When I stepped for the first time onto that wooded New Hampshire campus, my sense of taste skewed irreversibly. At the center of the quad loomed a beautiful gothic cathedral that was, as Curtis Sittenfeld describes in her novel *Prep*, called a chapel only out of Yankee modesty. Boarding school was fancy like the worn burgundy leather on the schoolhouse sofas, the names of alumni engraved on the wooden walls of the dining hall and appended with III and IV and V, an elegance that is inimitable because it is lived in. It was tradition to rub the names of your relatives as you walked past, and on some names the mahogany had been burnished, over decades, to a gleam. My dorm was a white cottage on a hill. My classmates were from Boston, Newport, Greenwich, Princeton. The school's dress code was best described as country club casual; uniforms were for Catholics and the British. Boys needed a collar but not a suit or tie. Girls could wear T-shirts so long as they were tailored. Denim could be worn so long as it wasn't ripped or blue. The hottest people on campus wore things I'd previously associated only with nerds and *Caddyshack*, grosgrain belts, cable sweaters, madras shorts, polo shirts. But a week into fall term, I found myself on the shuttle bus to the mall. I bought some polos at

Old Navy, only to realize that the type of polo mattered too—
you could tell by the animal embroidered above the breast.
Sixty-five dollars for a shirt . . . my mom muttered on the phone.
Don't they sell those at Marshall's? My classmates' first names
were Cord and Bayard and Win and Phoebe and their last
names were on libraries. They played lacrosse and rowed crew,
didn't gnaw at their fingers or roll their eyes when they talked
to adults. They weren't glossy and cruel like the rich people on
Gossip Girl. They were windblown, affable. The primary char-
acteristic that seemed to define them was ease. In no sense was
I underprivileged: I was white and wealthy, privately educated.
If you zoomed out even a little, my classmates and I had almost
exactly the same things, but there, with my nose pressed up
against the glass, I saw that they had something else. At night,
I'd choose a popular kid from the school directory and google their last name plus their hometown, which would usually
yield their parents, which would in turn yield *New York Times*
wedding announcements and real estate listings and endow-
ments. They had ancestors who'd come over on the Mayflower,
old patinaed ivy-covered wealth and dads who'd never dream
of bragging. What they had was born of money, but money
alone couldn't buy it.

   The phrase *boarding school* connotes both glamour and
severity, but it's also exactly what it sounds like: a high school
where you aren't allowed to leave. Early on, I learned that I
was not the kind of student the faculty liked. At my tiny Mon-
tessori school, I'd been brash, funny, and smart, loved by my
tight-knit group of classmates. At St. Paul's, I was doughy and
sweaty, sassy not in a charming way but in a sullen, pinched

way. I was unable to finish assignments, incapable of banter, so prone to rolling my eyes that I did it without realizing. By October, the head of my dorm had threatened to suspend me for not cleaning my room enough. By February, my physics teacher had emailed me my midyear grade—67—and instead of hitting the Forward button to vent about it to my friend, I'd accidentally replied, with just one word: *FUCK*. I felt wary of the faculty at the school, in part because many of them seemed nearly identical to the students, and in part because they had the ability, at any hour, to get me into trouble—for checking in ten minutes late for curfew, for skipping chapel, for skipping field hockey, and most often, for skipping seated meal, the mandatory twice-weekly dinner in which all the students and faculty dressed up and sat at assigned tables to eat vaguely elevated food, like roasted Cornish game hens, or chicken cordon bleu. The stated purpose of the meal was community-building, but with the girls bantering in pastel dresses, the boys shaking hands in tweed jackets, everyone having seemingly practiced for this their whole lives, it felt suspiciously like a networking luncheon, or maybe a debutante ball.

Come spring, I was spiraling, until one Saturday in May, when it started to rain. Girls walked to the dining hall in rubber boots that cost $150. In the rector's living room, students ate fresh lemon poppy-seed cake and played board games as their bright anoraks hung on pegs in the foyer. Overnight, the rain failed to stop and became a flood, which by Sunday morning required an all-school emergency meeting, and by Sunday evening had ripped through the scenic campus, submerging cars, collapsing asphalt, and forcing us all to evacuate, a month before final exams. Suddenly, the year was over, a pardon so improbable that it seemed divine. I was allowed to go home.

When I returned in September for my sophomore year, nothing had changed, and this time, no flood came to relieve me. I barely left my room, which stank of discarded Lean Pockets crisping sleeves and dirty clothes. The only adults I trusted were the service staff, because they weren't there to monitor or enrich me, but simply to do a job. I got the sense that they liked me, or at least noticed with empathy the fact that I didn't fit in. There was nurse Sharon, who dispensed my newly prescribed Zoloft dose and pretended to believe me each time I showed up complaining of stomach pains and asking to skip class. There was Tina, who ran the campus snack bar and told me which things on the menu I should try. There was Joe, with an enormous beard and thick silver hoops in his ears, who ran the little stone hut that functioned as our post office. When I desperately began to order preppy accoutrements, it was he who fielded the packages, handing them to me with a grumpy sternness whose trace amounts of affection I relished, since I was reminded of my dad. Joe's wife, Suzanne, worked at the school store, where I'd go after class to buy candy bars and Vitaminwater and abscond to my dorm room to devour them.

Each finals week, I'd stay awake for three feverish days. Once the last exam was turned in, I'd throw a pile of dirty clothes into my suitcase and shuffle to Last Night Service where, on the evening before we all departed, the students would gather one more time. The chapel glowed like a candle against the starflecked sky. The bishop would say lofty words about fellowship or stewardship, but this wasn't what I came for. The students would hug their long list of goodbyes, but this wasn't what I came for either. All I wanted to hear was the Last Night Hymn. It was the same one every time. At the end of the service, on the organist's cue, five hundred of us sang of ceaseless streams of mercy, sacred pleasure and redeeming love, a stranger who'd wandered from the fold now redeemed, in life, and exhorting God, at death, to bring him to his heavenly home. Home was where I'd have to answer for my failures at school. Home was where an adult's disappointment was Irish Catholic yelling, not an Anglican furrow. But for three sung minutes, going home did seem heavenly, not because it offered love or pleasure, but simply because it was where I could rest.

As my grades plummeted and my absences piled up, my parents threatened to pull me out of school, but I begged them not to. I was miserable, but if I could just grit my teeth, it would be my name, and not my misery, that they'd engrave on the old wood walls. If I left, the misery would be mine to take with me. In April, my advisor called me into his study. It reminded me of a room from Clue. I sat in a padded leather chair and wondered if he'd read all the books on the shelves. He cleared his throat and looked down at the faded rug. He was sorry to tell me that there had been a conference call. It was clear that the school was no longer a good fit, and I'd been asked to leave. Through sobs, I started to beg, but the plane ticket had already been paid for. I was leaving tomorrow morning. My mom could come later to pack up my room.

When I got back to Illinois, the first thing I did was sleep for two days. The second thing, after I padded downstairs into the living room, was argue with my dad. Boarding school had

been his idea. I was the third of his children to attend one of
these schools and the third to hate it. I demanded to know why
he kept insisting we go. But hating it, he said, was the point.

When he arrived at his Ivy League campus in 1978, he
had seen boarding schools only in horror movies. But he
noticed, quickly, that his classmates already seemed to know
one another, or if they didn't know one another, they knew
about one another. Dotted throughout the Northeast, he
learned, were these mini-Yales, mini-Harvards, where, only
decades ago, students would hand the headmaster a slip of
paper containing the name of the college they wanted to
attend. A week into the semester, my dad called my grandma.
He was in over his head; he'd never been around so many
rich people. Some of them were city rich, and some of them
were WASP rich, and a lot of them were actually not rich,
but everybody seemed to know something he didn't. There
were two other Iowans: one whose dad was a surgeon, and
one whose dad was a professor. My dad's dad did just fine for
himself owning a gas station in Storm Lake, but he still wore
boots to work. *Back home you're fancy if you get braces*, he told
his mom, *but everyone here has a nose job and an analyst.* When
someone offered him coke, he thought they meant soda. He
begged to transfer to Iowa State.

But that part of his story came only later, from my grandma.
In the living room, when I asked him what he meant when
he said hating it was the point, he just answered my question
with one of his own. *Do you know what I did when I hated it?*
he asked. He waited until I muttered *What*, and then smiled,

sweeping his arms across the living room, which was anchored by a giant TV and a surround-sound setup. *I won.*

He and I had different ideas of winning. My classmates had something I wanted, but it wasn't money. I'd begun to suspect it wasn't their Anglican pedigrees either. More than their clothes, their nicknames, their knowledge of skiing, what I wanted to win was their winning, their mastery of idiom. I wanted an idiom to master.

———

In my childhood bedroom, bored and lonelier than ever, I got a Tumblr account. I'd failed at being preppy, so I dedicated myself to mapping the tastes of hip urbanites instead. They were, in some ways, trickier than WASPs. WASP tastes were fixed, impervious to the fluctuations of mass culture—this became clear when I bought a copy of *The Official Preppy Handbook* on eBay, published in 1980, and saw that WASPs had worn (critter-print pants), eaten (creamed spinach), and listened to (Cat Stevens) more or less the same things for decades. The urban hip, though, were gluttons for culture and stood at its forefront, their tastes a carefully curated mix of high and low, new and old. *The Hipster Handbook*, which I also bought, was published in 2003 and delineated a set of overlapping but distinct subgroups whose allegiances split and converged constantly. Some wore overalls and some wore designer jumpsuits. Some drank cheap beer and some drank expensive bourbon. Some of them had money, but many did not, and the beer or the bourbon wouldn't tell you who was who. Class certainly played a role in their identity, but it did not determine it. If preppiness was like the aristocracy, its hierarchies straightforward but impenetrable, then hipness was like the stock market; technically, anybody could play, but you had to learn its rules, which were as byzantine as they were mutable. WASP culture was so homogeneous and assured of its power that its rules were rarely spoken of, nor enforced. Hipsters had no such ease. They cared very much about the rules. When you went to post on Tumblr, it displayed the same default text every time. It was a conversation between a tourist and a local in New York City, the capital of cool. The tourist asked the local to point her toward the Times Square Olive Garden, to which the local replied *No, but I could give you directions to an actual Italian restaurant.*

The Olive Garden was my favorite restaurant. I grew up eating there. If you've paid attention to the American suburban mallscape, you'll notice that all Olive Garden restaurants can be roughly divided into two architectural styles: the elegant Italian villas with cobblestone walls that the company features in advertisements, and the small buildings with tan stucco that probably used to be something else. My hometown's OG was the latter, and the first time I saw the fancier villa style, I was on a spring-break trip to Orlando, where every chain restaurant is at the top of its game, flagship level. I remember walking up to it in the heavy evening heat. Topiaries and tall trees lined the path to the door, and families sat on carved limestone benches as they waited for their pagers to buzz. For months after that night, I'd speak wistfully of *the fancy Olive Garden.* More than Disney, more than waterslides, more than technicolor souvenirs, it was this vacation memory that I savored like a sweet, sneaking it out in quiet moments to nibble the edges. The villa was a paradise, which is to say, an escape.

I loved the food, all of it. I loved all five of their entrées alfredo. I loved the spinach artichoke appetizer like dippable soup. I loved the rug of crispy mozzarella hugging the five-cheese ziti al forno, the granules of parmesan flecking my spaghetti marinara, the silky-spongy tiramisu. Most of all, I loved the breadsticks. Unlike a batch of homemade breadsticks, which inevitably vary in shape and degree of toast, Olive Garden's breadsticks were identical, pale beige, oil-shined pillows of dough whose surface was unpocked by imperfection and unblemished by seasoning, save for a sprinkling of garlic salt. You could stack them in perfect towers, like Jenga blocks. They had little to no crunch, no sharp burnt corners, just an expanse of unrefined gluten that could easily fill your belly before the entrées even arrived. I loved the yellow lamps and the bouncy booths and the little decorative balcony that hovered above everything. It contained a bistro table and two curly metal chairs, but with no entrance or exit, its permanent emptiness took on the quality of reverence, like the tomb of the unknown soldier, a monument to the act of eating at the Olive Garden.

Pundits talk a lot about red and blue states, about rural and urban, about the heartland and the "coastal elites," but one ideological divide has gone largely unexplored: that of people who would be embarrassed to have dinner at the Olive Garden, and people who would not. Of course, one could argue that eating at the Olive Garden is not, in fact, an ideological position but a socioeconomic one. People's tastes tend to align with what they can afford, so sit-down chain restaurants tend to be, generally speaking, not for the poor or the rich, but for the middle class. But one would be wrong. It's true that *how often* one eats at the Olive Garden is a matter of money, but whether one would eat there at all is indicative of something else entirely. The hipsters were clearly embarrassed. The WASPs would be embarrassed and baffled. My family would feel right at home. Would I?

These questions of taste were new to me. I tried to determine what part of the Olive Garden most rankled the elite. It was a chain that served unhealthy, cheap food, but none of those things on its own seemed to explain its status. I was familiar with the concept of a guilty pleasure. In the early 2000s, eating fast food carried a degree of guilt, but rarely was the pleasure itself taboo. Corporations were bad for America, and junk food was bad for your body, but few questioned the fact that McDonald's and Taco Bell tasted good. Unhealthy food was a vice, but vices were sordid and a little sexy, and so they were OK, in small doses at least. Olive Garden was no vice.

Nor did the chain part explain the embarrassment. Hipsters ate at sit-down chains every so often, like Denny's and Golden Corral. To eat a smiley-face breakfast pancake was kitschy and silly, not embarrassing. The Olive Garden was not quick and dirty, nor cheap and campy. It wasn't lurid, or elegant, or niche. In fact, it was a little bit of everything, and so it wasn't much of anything at all. Olive Garden customers weren't eating there because of what it said about them. They didn't think it comically bad, nor did they think it pinky-out fancy. They just liked it. They liked it just fine. Other chains were cheap in both

37

cost and aesthetics, and they held no illusions about themselves. They were in on the joke. Olive Garden, on the other hand, took its mediocrity seriously.

Taking one's mediocrity seriously is the hallmark of the middlebrow, a stratum of culture with which the Olive Garden has long been synonymous. In a 1941 open letter that never got sent, Virginia Woolf railed against the middlebrows. Highbrows were wealthy intellectuals whose lives were dedicated wholly to the proliferation of thought and art. Lowbrows were vigorous commoners whose lives were dedicated to labor. Woolf celebrated both the high- and the lowbrows for their singularity of purpose. She reserved all her scorn for middlebrows. Middlebrows were strivers who sidled up to both high and low, aspiring to the rarefied tastes of one and the proletarian authenticity of the other. In attempting to be both, they ended up being nothing. Hers was the age-old position of the WASP: you can only be what you always were. It's unseemly to aim.

It is easy to assume that Woolf saw the brows as wholly synonymous with socioeconomics because she identified, correctly, that culture and capital are linked: it's easier to make and access art when you have money. In her lifetime, though, taste was rapidly unhooking itself from class. Class in England was seen as an ancient and fixed apparatus until the mid-1800s, when people began to make quick, big money through industry and commerce. They could mingle with the landed gentry at parties and even buy their land. But they couldn't buy their taste. When Woolf decried the middlebrows, she sneered that they lived in South Kensington while the highbrows lived in Bloomsbury—but Kensington was the richer one. Woolf herself grew up there, moving to Bloomsbury when she was an adult, not because it was fancier, but because it was less so. Money and culture were now separate economies, or at least, they were incompletely conjoined. Woolf defined the middlebrows not by how much money they had, but by how proficiently they consumed.

———

In the end, my dad stayed in the Ivy League. He swore to retaliate against rich assholes and redistribute the wealth, which he did, by becoming an entirely different type of rich asshole. He loves NASCAR and hates New York City. To flout the limousine liberals, he became a MAGA Republican who watches *The Big Bang Theory* and *Two and a Half Men*. His bookshelves provide only information and rote instruction: glossy weight-lifting tomes, thick keto bibles, the authorized biography of Ronald Reagan. The only titles you'd see in a college classroom are the *Critique of Pure Reason*, Kant being the lone intellectual token he grants himself, and a tiny, pocket-size copy of Sun Tzu's *The Art of War*. His favorite television character has always been Jed Clampett, a poor mountaineer who got rich but never liked rich people. Jed hit oil while shooting a rabbit and moved his family to Beverly Hills, where his neighbors gawked at the pigs and chickens in his yard. It was never clear to me why Jed moved to Beverly Hills in the first place—he never seemed to like it, always missed home, clashed with his blue-blooded Bostonian neighbor, Mr. Drysdale. Jed's house got nicer, but he didn't change at all. He didn't want to. Some of my friends have artsy parents who are rich in culture, professorial types who own volumes of poetry and no television, and they would never even think to eat at the Olive Garden. My dad gave up on a pedigree. He took the money and ran.

In the end, I went back to boarding school. I hated my last two years just as much as my first two, but I didn't want to be a WASP anymore. I spent most of my time in my room, on Tumblr, fantasizing about college—a prepackaged coming-of-age experience from which I could emerge cooler, wiser, and ready to move to New York, where I now dreamed of living. Money could still buy that.

Soon after I graduated college, a group of activist investors staged a coup of the Olive Garden. In a three-hundred-page report, they outlined everything the chain was doing wrong. Olive Garden was not fresh. It was greasy, oversauced, under-seasoned, strangely sweet. Olive Garden was inauthentic. Like all chains, it blanched the flavor out of any culture it touched and gave birth to strange, pale chimeras whom it christened with names like *Pasta Diablo* and *Angry Alfredo*. It took every dish and fried it for no reason. Most galling was this: the Olive Garden didn't even salt the pasta water. When the investors' report made headlines, people assumed that this policy was the result of ignorance; salting the pasta water is Cooking 101. In the past decade, I've noticed that instructions to salt the pasta water, once doled out in earnest to the uninitiated, have taken on an incredulous, exasperated dimension in many cooking shows and recipes, a tone of *Please for the love of god, it should go without saying.* To leave your pasta water unsalted is to admit

one of two equally appalling things: that you live in a cave and
don't even realize it, or that you know you live in the cave, and
you like it there. As a matter of fact, Olive Garden did know
that salting the pasta water makes it taste better. Of course the
restaurant knew this. But it also knew that salt shortened the
warranty on all that industrial cookware, and most important, it knew what its customers did and did not care about. To
this day, OG still doesn't salt the pasta water. After reading the
report, I began to salt mine, and it might've tasted better, but I
couldn't really tell. Though I now knew what better was, I still
wasn't sure I cared.

Woolf disdained middlebrows in part because they looked
to other people to dictate their tastes. They saw taste as a com-
modity rather than an earnest and personal response to culture.
By contrast, she said, *We highbrows read what we like and do what
we like and praise what we like.* An editorial in *Punch* magazine
around the same time called middlebrows *people who are hoping
that someday they will get used to the stuff they ought to like.*

Woolf seemed to think that the *like* was taste and the *ought*
was posturing, but these have always been the two prongs of
taste. First, whether you like something, which has nothing to
do with quality and everything to do with pleasure. Second,
whether you think it's good, which is to say, whether you recognize in it certain markers of quality. Woolf's middlebrows
knew what they ought to like, but could not bring themselves to
actually *like* it, because the liking is all body, and the knowing is
all brain. Or really, they're both brain: the liking must answer to
the knowing, the brain of *ought* tugging pleasure from its warm
cave. Through high school and college, I noticed my cultural

attitudes changing, but I couldn't tell which brain was driving. When I first began my pursuit of coolness in high school, I loved the Olive Garden and thought it was good. By the time I entered graduate school, three-quarters of what I watched, listened to, read, and ate was a mix of pomp and camp that fit the profile of a cool person, but I felt sheepish about the last quarter. I still loved *The Da Vinci Code*. I still loved the wrong eras of country music. And though I had been trained to recognize its flaws, I still loved the Olive Garden. So, like any sheepish intellectual, like any good Catholic, I enshrined my guilt. I constructed a narrative in which everyone around me was a snob to the middlebrow and I its brave advocate. In graduate school, I wrote an essay in which I defended not just my own enjoyment of the Olive Garden but the enjoyment of the masses. I reiterated again and again how mediocre the food was while also defending my right to savor it. *Taste is a farce*, I declared at the end, and when I read my manifesto aloud to a room full of writers, I delivered it with all the passion of a stump speech.

Why then, when I visited my parents, did I still take taste so seriously? *Why don't you try* The Wire? I asked as one CBS sitcom rolled into the other, *Or* The Sopranos, I pressed on, *it's much better*. In pestering my dad to change his media diet, I imagined that I was enriching him, guiding him gently out of laugh-tracked TV and into the realm of gritty prestige. Instead, he stared ahead, jovially, and said *I like this*. I realized, then, the perfection of his argument. He liked what he liked, but I was still striving.

The more I tried to define middlebrow, the more I learned that its precise borders had been a cultural battleground for nearly a century. Twenty years after Woolf defined the middlebrow, Dwight Macdonald coined the term *midcult*, defining middle culture by its aspirations to universality. Midcult lay between avant-garde and schlock, broadly likable, smart enough to feel elevated, bland enough to not challenge your palate. Things I'd assumed fancy (Gothic Revival architecture, an Ernest Hemingway novel) were apparently midcult. I felt lost. I saw one critic declare Oprah's Book Club the middlebrow, while another named *The New Yorker*. I learned that television shows I saw as gritty prestige had been cited by one writer as prime examples of middlebrow television, of which we were said to be in a golden age. Some critics declared middlebrow to no longer be a pejorative, while others insisted cultural hierarchies were over altogether, that we had no brows left. What's more: I had misunderstood Woolf's letter all along. It had not been an unprovoked attack on middlebrow taste, but rather a defense of her own. A critic had eviscerated her most recent book and the group of highbrows to which she belonged, calling them *terrifically sensitive, cultured, invalidish ladies with private means*. He proudly identified as a *broadbrow*, his definitions of broad- and highbrows the reverse of Woolf's: it was *broadbrows* who liked what they liked, and highbrows who pretended. The critic was not an underdog, though; he was a writer whose mass appeal had made him much richer than Woolf. He was ashamed by his own palatability, and so he'd sharpened his artistic anxieties into a spear, called the spear her pretension, and thrust it into her hands. And she was right, he ought to be embarrassed.

Wealth and culture had been put in a blender, and we all swam in the same soup. The only brow that seemed to

remain, the only one there'd ever been, was the small, furrowed one that still cared to debate its own meaning. Professional athletes with Rolexes were spending ten grand at
the Cheesecake Factory. Warren Buffett was eating like a six-
year-old. Liberal arts college graduates wore thrifted Carhartt
and used food stamps at the co-op. A Gucci belt made you
look either richer or poorer, depending on who you asked.
Reality TV was being taught at universities, and it seemed,
at this point, more puerile to disdain it than to accept its
undeniable delights. Even my stuffy old boarding school had
started letting students wear blue jeans. If taste still conferred
cultural prestige, then there were so many different subsets
of prestige, so many different gods to pray to, that to pursue
or even acknowledge any particular form of prestige was a
sign that you already had it. If you strove to be part of the
club, it meant you were already in it. In school, one of my
professors remarked that her taste buds had changed as she'd
gotten older; her tolerance for sweetness ebbed as her desire
for acrid, challenging flavors sharpened. I was skeptical until
it began happening to me. I could eat only a few bites of a
sugary dessert before putting it down. I had to dilute juice
with water. I began to love olives, IPAs, black coffee, raw fish.
I went back to the Olive Garden a few times, but each time
I enjoyed it less. The five-cheese ziti al forno was somehow
both under- and oversalted. The breadsticks were a little too
bready. Had learning the pleasure of more rarefied flavors
genuinely inured me to the pleasure of simpler ones? Or had
my critical brain become so convinced of the Olive Garden's
mediocrity that it eventually tricked my animal brain into

following suit? I was finally getting used to the things I ought to like. Whether or not I'd meant to, I was crossing over.

I continued to confess my love for OG as if it were a risky statement, as if people would clutch their pearls. *The food might be bad*, I'd offer, raising an eyebrow, *but I love it*. Most often, though, people would agree with me. *Totally*, they'd smile, *the breadsticks rule*. As it turned out, a lot of people liked the Olive Garden. The multibillion-dollar chain was, in fact, quite popular. Only very occasionally did the imaginary snobs against whom I'd railed actually materialize in front of me, and on these occasions, I felt relief, not anger. Rarely did I encounter a foe who could validate my own smug, facile position. It's why the Westboro Baptist Church is so successful; only the campy villainy of GOD HATES FAGS could make something as flaccid as LOVE WINS seem revolutionary.

As I ran out of things to bang my fist on, it became clear that my first mistake had been banging my fist at all. When a North Dakota newspaper columnist wrote an earnest, mild review of the restaurant—*The chicken alfredo was warm and comforting on a cold day*—the voices that mocked her were quickly drowned out by the voices of righteous populism. She became a folk hero and soon published a book. Her review wasn't a rave, nor an impassioned defense of the restaurant; it was sensational because she presented her enjoyment without caveat. Meanwhile, while I professed to be making a farce of taste, I was still following taste's lone remaining edict: you could like bad things without embarrassment, so long as you conceded their badness. You could sin, as long as you made clear which god you prayed to. The truth is, most of the people who eat at the Olive Garden wouldn't think it in need of defending in the first place. It's just a nice place to go with your family on a Friday, no ironic wink, no puffed-up theories, no ornate apologia necessary. By escorting Olive Garden into the realm of acceptability, I'd revealed my belief that such a realm existed, and that I was one of its gatekeepers. True iconoclasm would've been my unqualified pleasure, but I couldn't unqualify my pleasure. I was in too deep.

A few years ago, my dad bought property at the top of a Carolina mountain, a gleaming modern farmhouse surrounded by acres of trees and tall grass. He then bought a fleet of farm vehicles and began leveling the land, not to plant crops or raise sheep, but to erect a shantytown of storage sheds and fill them with more vehicles, more implements. When I came to visit, I found my younger sister scrolling Instagram on the porch. *He's out box blading,* she shrugged, *and listening to country radio.* She gestured down the hill, where he was driving a tractor in merry circles. *He's so happy,* she continued. *It's like Marie Antoinette when she built the fake peasant village.* Strewn through the yard were trailers and side-by-sides and ATVs. Parked in the gravel driveway were two pickup trucks: one for pulling new tractors up the mountain, and one for hauling trash down to the landfill. In the living room, a giant TV perched above the stone hearth with a football game on, and in the kitchen there was a separate beverage fridge and a separate meat freezer and a separate ice maker that made those good restaurant cubes, and in case the fridge ran out of room, six of the fanciest coolers money could buy sat on the wraparound porch, filled with cases of beer and every color of Monster Energy drink. In his fantasy, he always has something to drink, and it's always as cold as he wants it. This, not the Beverly Hills mansion, was where Jed Clampett would put his oil money.

And I? I left Iowa and finally made it to New York. The oil had already been struck for me, the wealth already attained, and so I was free to continue my quest toward acculturation. The day I arrived, I arranged to meet a friend for lunch. She was from Queens, so I deferred to her, asking if there was a place she liked near her work. *I was craving Pizza Hut the other day . . .* she texted, and I responded . . . *I would.* I always would. In a windowless, low-ceilinged food court inside Penn Station, sandwiched between a KFC, a Häagen-Dazs, and a Taco Bell, we hugged and sat down to share a personal pizza. When I mentioned it later to another friend—she was also from Queens—I anticipated disapproval. The world's best slice could be had for a song in New York City, whereas even in the tiny Iowa town where we'd all gone to college, where the only other pizza place was the gas station, Pizza Hut had ranked a pitiful second. But my friend shrugged. *Doing what can only be done here is for transplants.*

By that point, I'd abandoned the idea that going to the Olive Garden made me a populist, but I still found myself there from time to time. To my dining companions, I'd note what had changed. When the server placed a basket of breadsticks on the table that equaled the number of diners plus one, I revealed that this was a policy enacted after the investor coup. The unlimited breadsticks, once refilled as automatically as your water glass, were now replenished only upon request. It saved the company millions. When the menu advertised a deal that allowed you to order two dinners at once, one to eat now and one to eat later, I explained that to-go was huge, and sit-down chains now did half their business at the curb. *Look at that redesign*, I'd say, pointing to their logo, which had morphed from loopy script on a Tuscan-stone background to a minimal version reminiscent of the fast-casual grain-bowl places I now frequented on my lunch breaks. I ordered some interchange-able pile of flour and dairy, and when we paid our bill on the touchscreen kiosk, I shook my head, because on top of not being that good, it wasn't even that cheap, and the man who admonished the tourist had been right after all: I'd rather have gone to an actual Italian restaurant.

It's not that I despised the food. It brought me about as much joy as a Lean Pocket, which I also still ate, propped up by pillows in my bed like an inpatient. But now, when I went to restaurants, I didn't want the comfort of bed. I wanted to share microgreens and oysters with a friend, a candle and a small bun-dle of wildflowers between us, and when I said I enjoyed it, it wasn't a lie. It was like banter at a party, a charming little mus-cle I was flexing, and it was nice to remind myself I could. But alone in my house with the foods I instinctively threw into my grocery basket time and time again—frozen chicken nuggets, Goldfish crackers, Uncrustables, Diet Snapple—my palate hadn't changed at all. I ate like my grandma, I ate like my brothers, I ate like a child, I ate like my dad. Stumbling to the kitchen at 3 a.m., I reached for Just Crack an Egg, a microwaveable plastic cup that promised an easy breakfast scramble. I could more easily and cheaply crack an egg in a pan and sprinkle on bacon bits and cheese, and some part of me knew this, but that part had gone dark. In me, hunger and psychic fatigue. In this, an ease so needless it became baroque. The product and I shared a blood-line. To call it my *taste* seemed beside the point. Familiarity was the place before pleasure, before knowing, before choice. What now drew me to the Olive Garden wasn't quite earnestness or irony. I felt duty-bound to bring people, like showing them my hometown. It felt as strange to hate it as to love it, as strange to return there as to not.

One March, after work, I took the train up to Midtown. Though I'd lived in New York half a year, I hadn't been back to Times Square since the ill-fated acid trip. A dead rat was lying on the sidewalk, and as I stood regarding it, waiting for my friends to join me, a live one ran across my shoes. I was standing in front of the Olive Garden. I had a gift card. In the eight years since I'd been there last, I'd taken acid one more time, and that dose was punishingly real. Personhood dissolved around me and life became a sensory goo. The only thing that tethered me back to linear time was a cheap gold chain that I balled in my fist for hours. Whatever I'd been on in Times Square hadn't been that, but I still wasn't sure that it had been nothing, because the sensory experience I'd found assaultive then seemed merely irritating now. At the time, I had won-dered whether tourists thought this was the "real" New York, whether they realized that they had come all this way just to be back in a midwestern mall. But now, I suspected that the tourists who flocked to Times Square were under no illusions to the contrary. They were, in fact, seeking exactly this. They wanted to see the familiar exalted, made holy by the powers declaring it so. Times Square was like going to the Vatican. People flocked there because of the other people who flocked there. I knew Times Square to be considered a grotesque symbol by anyone who considers themselves a person of taste, but standing there, I realized it was grotesque only in the way anything familiar is when magnified, like a knuckle under a microscope, an unremarkable expanse suddenly transformed into a monstrous inflamed network of oil and fur.

Zoom out from the monstrous knuckle and it becomes just a knuckle. Zoom out again, it becomes a hand, a body, a planet, a field of galactic dust, attached to nothing and everything. Freed from its associations and reduced to mouthfeel, *olive garden* is a sumptuous phrase, like *mountain dew* or *hidden valley*. Say it a few times aloud, and you forget the restaurant. Say it a few more times, and it loses all meaning. You can summon everything at once: sun-bleached stone and warm yellow walls, plush grasses, pillowed booths, incandescence, the smell of bread, the smell of oils, the smell of a fruit that is said to be holy. Chain restaurants are soothing because they are the same everywhere, like hymns.

Live, Laugh, Lose

THE NIGHT BEFORE I WENT to fat camp, I ate my last meal at an Olive Garden in Whitehall, Pennsylvania. My mom and I had flown there that day from the Chicago suburbs. I was seventeen years old and had flown alone plenty of times. I went to boarding school a dozen states away, so the ritual of parting with a parent outside an airport door was so familiar to me it had become quotidian. Still, my mom's presence was never a question. I needed her there.

The nice thing about loving chains is that your favorite restaurant is everywhere. Allentown had many of my favorites: Applebee's, Red Robin, Denny's, and even an On the Border Mexican Grill. But I knew, without thinking, where we would go.

We ordered an appetizer sampler with zucchini, lasagna, and mozzarella, fried and indistinguishable from one another. *I wonder what you're going to eat there*, my mom mused as I dipped a breaded stick in marinara. *They'll probably make you eat a lot of green stuff.*

My mom and I have never shared the same taste in food. She is, without a trace of disorder, an intuitive eater, which is to say, the foods she wants to eat and the foods she needs to eat are one and the same. If she goes too long without a vegetable, a small sensor in her brain will make her crave one. If a dessert is too sweet, that same sensor will determine the perfect number of bites. She never has to restrict. She never has to pine. She never has to regret. She is constitutionally moderate.

I was not like her. When she wanted fast food, she'd get herself a small McDonald's fry and a cheeseburger and feel perfectly content. When I wanted fast food, I wanted three Arby's sandwiches dripping in cheddar sauce. Her pizza was a thin crust veggie, mine a stuffed crust with extra meat. If she wanted to go to LongHorn, a chain that mostly serves straightforward steaks and baked potatoes, then I wanted the Cheesecake Factory, a chain whose menu is twenty-five pages long and includes a section called Glamburgers. Like me, she enjoyed chain restaurants, but I was always occupying the saltier, tackier, simpler, and more gluttonous niche.

In the witching hour between school and dinner, I'd devour the kind of desperate, feral meals that only a fat child would understand: cream cheese on a spoon, a blanket of Kraft Singles melted over popcorn, rolls dipped in ranch, four cold hot dogs eaten standing up in front of the open fridge. *It wouldn't matter if your stomach was 99 percent full*, my dad observed. *You'd still see the 1 percent as hunger.* I'm loath to ascribe anguish, or boredom, or really any emotion at all to how or why a person gets fat. We know by now that the reasons are far more arbitrary than previously believed, or rather, that they are not arbitrary at all, but such a complex and intangible thicket of biology and circumstance that any attempt to divine them reads more like moralistic soothsaying than anything else. I don't know exactly why I was so hungry then, but I know that every bite felt stolen.

I was also picky. The foods I relished were mostly shades of beige.

Most people assume that pickiness is an aversion to new flavors, but it often has little to do with taste. Pickiness stretches back to the beginning of our lives, when the world of food is astounding, and we rate each new bite not by taste but by texture. We learn to touch that way. After this period of curiosity, many babies enter the neophobic stage. They become protective of their mouths. They will hate brushing their teeth and will pack chewed food in their cheeks until they absolutely must swallow.

The neophobic stage is supposed to end at age six or seven, but some people retain that sensitivity to texture into adolescence, adulthood, even. The foods that the picky hate feel strange on the tongue. They are slippery, mushy, membranous, leaky, full of bones and seeds and gristle. They threaten a dark wetness beneath their flesh. For a long time, I wouldn't touch eggs, pickles, grapes, citrus, plums, most fruits, in fact, besides apples and bananas. I tolerated cucumbers and carrots but not artichokes or corn on the cob. I would not eat chicken wings or ribs, only nuggets. Even foods I liked were landmines, like in preschool when I eagerly grabbed for a chocolate chip pancake at a special class breakfast and retched when I bit down instead on the sour goo of a blueberry. I couldn't stand the tiny, chopped onions on a McDonald's hamburger, the cherry on a sundae, or the chunks of tomato that lurked in a brick-oven pizza. Raw tomatoes are enemy number one for picky eaters.

From the outside, tomatoes look innocent, like apples. Bite into an apple and it stays simple, a singular crispness. Tomatoes look simple, but the smoothness of their skin belies a slimy web of innards too complicated for my blind tongue to parse. That's what I fear about my mouth: its blindness.

At seventeen, at the Allentown Olive Garden, I still had a child's soft brain. I was clenched in every way, bracing myself against something I couldn't name. So I preferred simple foods. Foods I loved because I trusted them, because they made me feel good, bread and cheese and sweetness and oil. The previous Thanksgiving, I'd refused what my mom had spent days preparing and sullenly sat at the table eating a tray of Bagel Bites. I'd gone on a trip to Japan and eaten only rice and candy. Every time I refused something, people would look at me incredulously. *Why can't you just try it?* I had no answer. The narrowness of my pleasure commanded shame.

After dinner, my mom and I went back to the hotel room and ordered *Atonement* on pay-per-view. We lay on separate beds, half watching the story of two lovers and the wars standing between them.

Are you nervous? she asked finally.

Yeah, I said, *but not really about the fat part.* And then, out of nowhere, I burst into tears.

It had been a long year. I'd been living at home after my boarding school had asked me to leave. Little had changed since then. On my first day at the local high school I'd begun attending, the principal assigned a buddy to show me around. Her name was also Emily. She seemed popular, not in the mean, haughty way you see in movies, just in the sense that she smelled good and knew everyone. I sat at her table for lunch, unpacking my brown bag with my turkey sandwich, saying nothing but smiling along as her friends chatted. The next day, I scanned the cafeteria nervously, my heart rate accelerating, and, knowing nobody but her, sat down at her table again. This continued for the rest of the week. I felt sheepish about my presence, knowing that Emily's allowing me to shadow her on the first day was the act of a dutiful student ambassador, not a friend, and that she probably hadn't bet on my sticking around. On the ninth day of school, I stayed up until 5 a.m. nervously ignoring a history assignment that ended up taking only twenty minutes to complete. I arrived late wearing a hastily thrown-on pair of my dad's basketball shorts and a hoodie, my hair in a greasy bun, my skin clammy. That was the first day I bought, rather than packed, my lunch. Again, I sat at Emily's table. The only sound coming from my mouth was the crunch of my Crispitos, taquitos filled with a meat-and-cheese goo so soft and homogeneous in texture that it could only have been extruded from an industrial tube. They reminded me of mollusks, but did not disgust me like mollusks, and anytime Crispitos were served, I ate a minimum of four. On the tenth day, it was Bosco Sticks, delicious pale puffy breadsticks stuffed with cheese, and Emily's table, again, and on the eleventh day, I knew there was no turning back. The year passed. Each day, I would buy a greasy little meal and sit hunched on the plastic stool that was attached to the round lunch table. The group would talk about boyfriend problems and sneaking liquor into prom, and I would stare at my tray. Each day my anxiety—at how lumpen and sullen an addition I was to this group of affable volleyball

players, at the unspoken strangeness of the arrangement, at my
inability to speak a word, to interject myself into even a single
conversation—was exceeded only by my anxiety at the thought
of trying to sit anywhere else. At least once a week, I would
stay in my bed and refuse to go to school, even when my mom
got so frustrated she called the police, who rang the doorbell a
few times before giving up and driving away. I received two in-
school suspensions. I kept wearing the basketball shorts and the
hoodies, marinating in my own salt and oil. My hair became so
matted that when I did muster the energy to shower, it took me
a half hour to detangle the knots. I got a C in gym and a D in
AP US history. I gained thirty pounds but it barely registered.
I flinched when someone brushed past me in the hallway, or
when my sweet sociology teacher touched my shoulder as we
wrote letters to our future selves, which she planned to send
back to us in five years. Under the goal section, I wrote *Happy?*
and *Finally cleaning room on a regular basis* and *Not dropped out.*
After the year I'd had, it wasn't the food or the exercise that
scared me about camp. It was everything else.

   We drove up in the rental car the next morning. The camp
was nestled along a narrow, tree-darkened road. We turned right
and the road suddenly opened up into 350 sprawling private
Pocono acres. Adults in sunglasses drove past on golf carts and
spoke into walkie-talkies and held clipboards. Kids waved and
hugged. It looked like a camp from the movies. Being seventeen
placed me in the oldest group of campers, the Super Seniors. We
occupied two cabins at the top of a steep hill, which led down
to the pool and the lake. After she had shaken hands with the
camp staff and signed a series of waivers, my mom accompanied

me into cabin J-14, where we were welcomed by Kristy, our
tanned and sturdy head counselor who was majoring in nutrition. She told me I was the first camper to arrive. *We're pumped
to have you here, Emily,* Kristy said with the buoyant kindness of
a team captain, *It's gonna be an awesome summer.* She turned to
my mom. Gently, as I'm sure she had been trained, she said, *I'll
take it from here.* We left Kristy in the cabin and said our goodbyes on the cabin steps. For most of my life, my mom and I had
not said I love you when we parted. Her parents' own reticence
had been passed on to her, and she had passed it on to me. We
were nervous. We didn't know how. But we said it this time as
we hugged, muttering it quickly into each other's shoulders. I
laid my cheek briefly against her back, my eyes welling up. Then
she was gone.

Back in the cabin, I unloaded the contents of my duffel
onto my bed (*NO bunk beds,* the camp brochure had boasted).
Kristy came over to watch me do it. *Sorry,* she explained, *they
just want us to make sure there's no outside food.* Into the shelv-
ing unit above my bed went twelve pairs of brightly colored
shorts, twelve baggy T-shirts, four pairs of spandex and four
long tank tops to layer under the shorts and T-shirts, an iPod
speaker, three sticks of deodorant, a dress for special occasions,
a cardigan to wear over the dress, a one-piece bathing suit with
a tummy-concealing wrap in the front, a copy of *Skinny Bitch,*
which told me to eat nothing, and a copy of *French Women
Don't Get Fat,* which revealed that I could eat whatever I
wanted as long as what I wanted was a single croissant savored
slowly on my balcony in the hazy morning light.

My bunkmates began to filter in. According to the news,

to live in America in 2007 was to be surrounded by fat people, but this was the first time in my life that this had actually happened. I'd been at camp only an hour, but already I'd lost count of all the cotton-shirted belly rolls, the moon faces. I began to feel more at ease. Camp made me wonder if it wasn't the act of meeting people that scared me so much as it was their thinness. My body felt like a ponytail someone could grab in a fight, an open vulnerability it would be best to conceal as well as possible. For this reason, all the fat people in the world felt like my secret allies.

I met Charlie first. She was from Florida, tall with a deep tan, and held her fat in a kind of sturdy, elegant way. She greeted me with such warmth and natural ease that I could tell, immediately, that she was beloved back home. As she unpacked, I took stock of her Longchamp tote bags, her grosgrain headbands, all things the girls at my boarding school wore. Were it not for her sweetness and the fact that she was a few sizes bigger than me, I would've been terrified.

Morgan was from Connecticut and played a lot of sports. Ellie was quiet and Canadian. Like me, she wore the men's basketball shorts that had become my uniform that year. They had come to represent the complete antithesis of athleticism, their very fibers embedded with the malaise of a sickbed. I'd left mine at home, trading them in for Soffe shorts, which represented hot girls. Kat was tattooed, wore a wifebeater, and had two boyfriends back home. Amelia was from New York and only a size 12 or so, but she was self-effacing and had IBS, so she felt like one of us. McKenna and Alana were even smaller than Amelia, a pair of long, lean, certifiable hotties, which was not entirely uncommon at the camp. People eyed these girls in the same way you'd eye a professional singer who entered a karaoke competition. Sure, we all shared the same goal, and sure, there weren't rules against this kind of thing, but they had ignored the tacit underdog requirement that held the whole fragile thing together. The thin girls were still our friends, but we resented their power.

The Super Seniors headed down the hill to our first meal. As we entered the mess hall, Kristy pointed to a salad bar in the middle of the room. *All right, guys. You can have as much as you want from there*, she said. *But everything else*, she gestured to the row of silver hotel pans glowing orange under heat lamps, manned by staff members in hairnets and aprons, *is one per person*.

———

Earlier that year, I'd started seeing a therapist. In one of our early sessions, which would end up being one of our last, she asked me questions about my weight, which led to questions about my diet, which forced me to list all the foods I liked, all of which were processed. At the end she remarked with an air of wonder, *It's interesting. You eat like a poor person.*

I didn't quite know what she meant. In my mind, processed food was a joy common to all, and the only difference between people was the degree to which they indulged or resisted. I knew there was shame in overindulging—it was why the world was cruel to fat people. I knew that the world was cruel to poor people too, but I had not thought to link the two. Poverty, to me, was not a matter of indulgence.

I continued to puzzle over this link between scarcity and

abundance. I learned what a food desert was and realized that I ate as if I lived in one. I learned that Congress was debating whether you should be able to buy soda with food stamps. That Los Angeles had banned the building of new fast-food restaurants, but only in the poorest regions of the city, which sounded about as effective as banning a single brand of cigarettes from a single grocery store. According to the news, low-income people were getting fat because they ate bad food, and they were eating this food because they couldn't get anything better, or because they *refused* the better food, or perhaps because they didn't even *know* about the better food, as if eating more French fries than green beans could only be a mark of destitution, or ignorance, and not simply a reasonable response to the taste of a French fry. I didn't doubt the role played by structural barriers—time, money, health care—but I also knew that I wanted for nothing and still ate this way. The opinion pieces were not wrong about food deserts, but they elided what was, to me, the most obvious reason anyone eats processed food: because it *feels* good. So exquisite is the chemical effect of simple carbohydrates that the billion-dollar industries dedicated to resisting them seem only to augment their power. What could match that rush? What besides a drug could ever flood my dopamine receptors as effectively as the first crystalline sip of a Slurpee, or a bite from a dense gas station brownie? No chicken breast, no brussels sprout, could ever give me so much pleasure. When my therapist said I ate like a poor person, she meant that I ate like someone who couldn't do any better. Someone who didn't know what they needed or couldn't obtain it. But I knew exactly what it took to make me feel good. This good felt far more urgent than what was good *for* me. I saw healthy food as a tithe that borrowed from my brain to pay my body. Even with every resource to do so, I rarely felt equipped to pay such a tax.

I'd assumed everyone was lying about healthy food, but apparently there were people who genuinely enjoyed grilled salmon. There were people who wouldn't eat dinosaur chicken nuggets even if there were no penalty to health. People who preferred fresh strawberries dabbed in a bit of sugar to the silky frosting and plush crumb of a Hostess cupcake. People who had never cut the corner from a pouch of Velveeta and squeezed it into their mouths like icing. People who had never even been tempted.

Camp food, as it turned out, was fine. It didn't challenge my starchy palate. It was what my mom's cookbooks called "kid-friendly," healthy but not too healthy. Every protein and vegetable was tempered by a sauce, or a bread, or a layer of part-skim mozzarella cheese. Barbecue chicken with potato wedges, pita pizza, a cassette-size piece of steak with broccoli florets, one omelet and one pancake and one small plastic cup of maple syrup, cheesecake that consisted of low-calorie instant pudding in a miniature graham cracker piecrust, a dessert so popular that each camper was given a recipe card, so they could make it at home. Counselors kept watch for any unauthorized second helpings, though nobody in my group attempted to sneak any extra portions. We were all too happy to comply.

Like every other camper, I had been on diets before, knew all about calories-in and calories-out, but the transaction had never seemed so simple, so clean. We'd all shuffled through Jenny Craig (strange little frozen meals), Medifast (strange little shelf-stable meals), Weight Watchers (your own meals but gamified), the Special K diet (cereal), the Atkins diet (meat). At camp, we didn't feel we were being starved because the hard part of dieting is never the hunger, the physical fact of eating less. It's the knowledge that you can always eat more. A diet demands constant self-monitoring, willpower, choice. My dad always told me my problem was that I couldn't delay gratification, which a diet demands you do again and again and again, in infinite small ways, in service of a biological phenomenon that you cannot see or feel. You hope that with each dessert you forgo or hamburger bun you sub with a lettuce wrap, a tiny part of your body will quietly combust, until one day in some hazy future, so much will be burned away that you will tug on your loose waistband and know, definitively, that you have vanquished yourself.

At camp, there were no decisions to be made. The only edible thing sold at the camp canteen was sugar-free gum. Someone else counted our calories, measured our portions, scooped our little scoops onto our paper plates, and locked the pantry when they were done. Someone else told us when to wake and when to sleep, when to push ourselves and when to ease off, when to fill our water bottles, when and exactly how much to snack. Every so often, the usual midafternoon snack of a clementine or a small bag of pretzels would be replaced by an ice cream bar, no sugar added, but still. The treats were always handed to us from the deck of the staff offices by the camp's assistant director, Bob, whose slightly elevated position above us as we clamored on the grass below would give the feeding frenzy a vaguely papal air. It wasn't until my fifth week, twenty-two pounds down, that I noticed the brand name on the blue-and-white cellophane wrapper I had been tearing off the whole time: Sweet Freedom.

What came as a shock to my system was all the movement. In most of America, walking is a wellness activity that must be undertaken deliberately, not a viable means of transportation. At camp, though, I was moving from morning until night, not just during exercise periods but in between: hustling to and from activities, climbing up the enormous hill to get to dinner, tidying up the cabin, taking long, lazy loops around the grounds in the lilac hours between dinner and the evening activity. My whole life, I'd had problems falling asleep, but at camp I felt my mind quiet the minute I slid into bed each night, finally prone. For the first time in my life, lying down felt like a novelty.

———

People assume that fat camp was forced upon me. And it's true that when my mom first suggested it, I was upset. Going to fat camp would certify *fat* as something I was, rather than a temporary affliction. But I also wanted badly to escape it. Finding the right camp was the trouble. Wellspring, a popular one with locations in California and Florida, was the first that we researched. Its program included cognitive behavioral therapy, one-on-one nutrition counseling, and classes on the psychology of eating. I imagined a group of chunky teenage girls in a circle of folding chairs, crying as they pinched their thighs. My mom and I both grimaced at the talk of *healing* and *growing*. Too medical, too feely.

Camp Shane was another popular option. Their advertise-
ment in the back of *Seventeen* magazine featured a photo of a
smiling boy in a pair of shorts that had become too big for him.
Camp Shane did not seem clinical or therapeutic, but it carried
a strange, metallic aura. It felt like the factory-farming of fat
camps, its motto *Live, Laugh, Lose.* I found Camp Pocono Trails
on my own after watching a documentary series that MTV
had made about the camp. It looked more or less normal, and
it embarrassed me the least. It would do the job.

Days at camp were delicious in their sameness. Wake up
at 7:45 to the crackling sound of Bob's thick Jersey accent
wafting from the speakers above girls' camp. Put on the same
interchangeable outfit of cotton, spandex, and rubber. Head
to the flagpole outside the mess hall and pledge allegiance
before filing in for breakfast. Aerobics in the big barn at 10,
led by Gina, who wore Jazzercise outfits and had us sweating
so much that after an hour we'd lay our damp bodies down on
the clay tennis courts and leave behind life-size crime-scene
silhouettes. Something more low-key at 11, maybe a craft or
a drama class, then lunch, free time, group activity, snack, then
a ropes course perhaps, or tubing on the lake. In the evening
came dinner, showers, bed, lights out. Sometimes there would
be dances in the rec hall and the Super Seniors would put on
our nice dresses and cardigans and form a giggling, eye-rolling
circle as Akon crooned over the darkened dance floor.

Every Sunday, we were weighed in the auditorium. The
camp's founder, Tony, personally attended the weigh-ins. Tony's
parents had run Weight Watchers camps in the '70s and '80s. It
was at his parents' camp that a young Tony had met his wife, a

fellow camper, and in their twenties the couple had founded their own line of fat camps. We entered the weigh-in room to find Tony at a foldout table. An industrial scale sat on the floor in front of him. *Ms. Mester, how you doin'?* Tony asked as I stepped onto the large white square, the number not visible to me but displayed to him on a small LED panel. *Emily,* he paused for a moment as I held my breath, *you're down five pounds this week. You,* he pointed for emphasis as I stepped off the scale, beaming, *should be very proud of yourself.*

When I try to describe fat camp to others, they wince with sympathy. It sounds barbaric, a hellish panopticon of body fascists prodding and measuring you, policing your plate. But it wasn't like that at all. Maybe it was because Tony's approach to weight loss was unsentimental and direct, more like a soccer coach or a mechanic than a frowning doctor. Maybe it was because many of the staff members were also fat or had once been. Maybe it was because for many of us, weight loss already consumed our minds but had until now been a private, embarrassed undertaking. I remember hiding my face as I entered a strip-mall Jenny Craig, asking my mom to order me a Diet Coke at restaurants and pretend it was hers. My fatness felt like a desperate secret I was trying, and failing, to keep. I had sworn my family to silence about camp, and my bunkmates too, who were forbidden from posting any camp photos of me on Facebook. But there, sweaty, sunburned, doing step aerobics with three hundred other fat kids in a crowded, cement-floored barn, I couldn't hide myself from anyone. It was the freest I'd ever felt.

The only non-diet book I brought with me was *Moose* by Stephanie Klein, a memoir of her time at a fat camp that sounded eerily like my own, right down to the enormous, punishing hill. Like me, Klein was a lush overeater, but she had grown tired of her hunger being dissected, furrowed at, addressed as a symptom of some deeper internal wound. This "fatnalysis," as she called it, was ultimately pointless. She loved food but not what it made her. Unlike other camps, Camp Pocono Trails offered little in the way of fatnalysis, and this regular-campness was, to me, a highlight, not an oversight.

The only gesture toward our fragile inner psyches was Be Your Best with Bobbie. One day after snack, apples in hand, we walked to the campfire circle in front of the mess hall and sat down on halved logs, facing a woman in her mid-sixties. *Welcome*, she said, adjusting the sunglasses perched on top of her head, *to Be Your Best with Bobbie. My name is Bobbie Schecter.* Bobbie was, with her ginger bob and her clinking bangles, the camp's self-esteem coach, a role she'd held for thirty years. Bobbie had self-esteem down to a science. Within a few minutes, she was counting off the steps on her fingers: *First, we're gonna ask "Is this in my best interest?"* We practiced saying it to ourselves. *Second, each morning, we're gonna look ourselves in the mirror, and give ourselves an UP.* We patted ourselves on the back.

Every so often, fat camp's regular-campness would crack. On the way to Bobbie's class that afternoon, we passed by a girl weeping on the sidelines of a kickball game. Breakdowns often happened in the margins, along the wall in the aerobics barn, on the edge of the pool. *Is there this much crying at regular camps?* I asked Alana. She thought for a second. *Well*, she responded in her California vowels, *most camps are for kids that are interested in the same thing, like them*—she gestured across the lake, where there was a teen sports camp. *The only thing we all have in common is that we want to lose weight.* Lots of our fellow campers were the hardy, cheerful, softball-team types you'd expect to find at any summer camp. Others, though, had come not for summer fun but in a grim bid of desperation. They had been forced by their parents, urged by their doctors, bullied out of school. Like most sleepaway camps, fat camp was expensive—about $1,000 a week—but unlike those camps, it promised something that caused many parents to take out loans, cancel vacations, dip into retirement plans. One girl in the twelve-to-fourteen division had written an essay to secure one of a handful of scholarships the camp offered. She'd talked about how people whispered when she walked down the street, and compared herself to a plump caterpillar waiting to break free.

In the American imagination, camp is a place of fun, lust, and friendship. Fat camp, on the other hand, is meant to solve a problem. You sweated in your problem, hauled your problem up and down the hill, warmed your problem by the campfire. We had all arrived at camp in the thrall of a singular god—weight loss—and had bonded with the ferocity of soldiers in a war.

The class ended with Bobbie teaching us a chant. *What are we going to do?* she asked us. *Accentuate the positive,* we mumbled, and she could tell our hearts weren't in it. Her voice became more fervent. She told us to say it louder. *ACC-EN-TUATE THE POS-IT-IVE,* we yelled, raising our thumbs to the sky. She gestured for us to continue. *ELIM-INATE THE NEGATIVE,* we bellowed, sweeping our hands side to side in front of us. *And don't mess,* she added, wagging her finger sternly, *with Mister In-Between.*

Self-esteem at fat camp was a fraught, if not futile,

endeavor. These crude chants simply confirmed it. The camp brochures were always careful to twin any claims of weight loss with the promise that camp was, above all, a place to feel good about yourself—THE BEST MENTAL AND PHYSICAL SHAPE OF YOUR LIFE was the camp's motto, which we'd yell along with Tony at pep talks. Self-esteem was touted as both a side effect of weight loss and a prerequisite. You needed one to get the other. People grimace at this when I tell them, the two promises striking them as contradictory, even sinister. How could you feel good about yourself in a place like that? But I think their real discomfort lies in the camp's honesty.

We all desperately wanted self-esteem, but we did not see it as a thing we could conjure at will—not with fatnalysis, not with mantras, not with a sticker above a sink that said *You Are Beautiful.* Every time I saw one in the wild, I thought bitterly, *How would you know?* The concept of self-esteem without thinness was years away from the mainstream, but even when it did come, it wasn't enough to untangle the contradiction. We *were* all trying to feel good about ourselves, had been clawing for years to find peace any way we could, but in the battle of wills between fat and the world, the world kept winning. Before acceding to the difficult, lifelong task of trying to change our minds, we were seeing, one last time, whether we couldn't just do the easier thing, and change our bodies instead.

That's what everyone else wanted too. On my mom's nightstand, when I went looking for my confiscated Game Boy or extra Halloween candy, I'd glimpse a stack of self-help books with titles like *Overcoming Childhood Obesity* and *Trim*

Kids. When I revisit family photos, I try to see myself through their eyes. My face is soft and round as a bagel.

The whole world, in fact, had taken a stake in my weight. Every few months, another news magazine would publish another obesity issue. *Newsweek* had babies holding fries, a balloon-like belly about to be pricked by a pin, a man in a wifebeater whose large stomach had been inflated like a globe and superimposed with a world map, a pudgy adolescent holding an ice cream cone with the headline FAT FOR LIFE? across his middle. *Time* had an almost identical cover, their fat boy standing on a skateboard as he held his ice cream cone. The headline: OUR SUPER-SIZED KIDS. In another *Time* cover, an outline of the United States had been flipped sideways so that it resembled a face in profile. The Southern protrusions of Texas and Florida were the lips and Alaska was a hamburger poised to enter their wide-open maw. *The Atlantic* featured a double-chinned Statue of Liberty.

This rhetoric easily blended with the political climate of the early 2000s to rebrand fatness, which had long been seen as a quiet personal failing, into a national epidemic. Fatness had become a convenient symbol of the totality of American greed. It, too, had become political. War was fat. Our dependence on oil was fat. Corporate tax cuts were fat. Red states were ignorant, and ignorance was deep-fried, cheap, ugly, and fat. In the years following 9/11, I learned how much the world hated America, and I remember this being a concern of left-leaning Americans, many of whom joked about claiming to be Canadian on vacations. While the world's hatred was ostensibly aimed at our virulent conservatism, our bloody, listless wars, this political stance

was interpreted as a cultural distaste for our crudeness, our lack
of refinement, our puffed cheeks, our grease. My political awareness at the time was dim, but it seemed to me that what shamed
us most was not the violence our country visited on the poor,
the marginalized, the foreign, the innocent. It was the fat. Fat
would be the doom of Western civilization. Fat was the American atrocity.

But it was still an atrocity of choice. Four years before I
went to camp, Morgan Spurlock's documentary *Super Size
Me* was released in theaters. I was thirteen, and I watched
the movie when it came out on DVD, the cover featuring a
panicked-looking Spurlock with his mouth gagged by French
fries. The movie begins with a voice-over by Spurlock: *Everything is bigger in America,* he says. Cue photos of Hummers, mansions, a Walmart supercenter, a really big cookie, *and finally*—he
pauses as the camera pans up to the body of a fat woman sitting
on a cooler at the beach, her ass swathed in purple Lycra and
spilling over the seat, her back to the camera—*the biggest people.*

The film was inspired by a lawsuit two teenagers had
brought against McDonald's: they said fast food made them
fat. Years earlier, smokers had won a landmark case against the
tobacco lobby, and the teenagers argued that fries were not
so different. The judge disagreed—the consequences of smoking had been hidden from consumers, but any idiot knew that
McDonald's made you fat. The teenagers made their choice.
The case was thrown out.

Had the obesity epidemic been framed as a proper atrocity,
wrought not by individuals but by a profiteering apparatus in
possession of the world's most advanced biochemical weapons,

then maybe I could've arrived more quickly at the admission that, yes, fast food was bad for you, and yes, it was best to avoid it, and yes, this was, for half the country, nigh on chemically impossible. But this wasn't the movie's legacy. What everyone remembers is Spurlock pinching his flab as his thin vegan girl-friend looks on in concern. He vomits with glee in a parking lot. He becomes bloated and pained. His dick goes soft. This is why McDonald's is evil, we learn. This is what it turns you into. Spurlock's critique is supposed to be aimed at capitalism, but if the McDonald's corporation is the villain he aims to put on trial, then fat people are the horrifying crime scene.

———

One morning, we went to consult the daily schedule and noticed that the scheduled afternoon activity, softball, had been crossed off. Kristy briefed us: two writers were working on a book, and they wanted to talk to us. We were uneasy all through aerobics, through lunch, wondering if we were stepping into our own magazine cover.

We filed into the focus-group room, which was actually the dance studio where we learned routines set to Flo Rida songs. Someone had arranged long tables into a square. The writers, both women, wore the same beaded glass jewelry as my former therapist. *Our book isn't about weight loss*, they quickly explained after introducing themselves, perhaps noticing the apprehension on our faces. *It's really more about body image.*

After we went around and shared our names, the writers—Annie and Sharon—handed us each a piece of paper. *This might seem a little funny*, said Annie, *but we want you all to draw a pic-*

ture of yourself. It doesn't need to be artistic, and you don't have to show it to anyone. Just draw what you see in the mirror. In unison, we whipped our heads around to look at the wall of mirrors behind us. The camp did not have many mirrors. There was one above the cabin sink that we clustered around sometimes, but it was too small to give a true picture of our shrinking bodies. We only caught glimpses, a change in the slope of our upper arms, our outer thighs, our chins. Or sometimes in clothes, T-shirts whose tight fabric we once had to tug away from our bellies, now draping over them with ease. Sometimes, one girl's fat pants became another girl's thin pants.

Morgan raised her hand. *Can we use the mirror to help?* A few of us nodded in agreement and looked to the writers. *Actually,* Sharon said gently, *we'd love it if you could try to draw from memory.* At this, we broke into grimaces. *I know, I know,* Annie interjected. *Just try.*

I closed my eyes and pictured my body in the mirror. I don't know why we say *the* mirror and not *a* mirror, using the definite article as if there exists a single, universal mirror into which we all gaze, like the sky or the abyss. Really, it was the mirrors, plural, that I imagined. There were many in my life, each containing a slightly different body that my brain had attempted to merge into a single cohesive image. At my parents' house, my naked body was located in the rectangular, white-framed mirror in my bathroom. I would stand and pull its hips back to make them look more like Mischa Barton's. In my dorm, my body hung on the back of the door in one of the narrow Walmart mirrors that makes you look somewhat skinnier than you actually are, both a defect and a feature. I liked but did not trust that body, so sometimes, late at night, I'd drag a step stool into the communal dorm bathroom and try to get a good look at my undistorted legs in the plate glass mirror that sat behind the sinks. If the sky was sufficiently dark and the room sufficiently light, a window could become a mirror in a pinch. My grandma had a little circular magnifying mirror she used to pluck the hairs on her upper lip, and there was an even more magnified one at the Hammacher Schlemmer store in downtown Chicago, where I discovered that there were tiny, dark hairs on the snub of my nose. Realizing I still hadn't drawn anything on the page, I tried to imagine every version of my body in a police lineup and thrilled at the idea of seeing its many facsimiles all lined up in front of me, not because I loved the way it looked, but because I desperately wanted to know what it looked like at all. *OK, go ahead and stop where you are*, Sharon said. I looked down to see I'd only drawn a head.

We went around the room. Several people had jokingly drawn stick figures with boobs. *They're the fattest part of me*, giggled Dede, a pretty Super Senior from the other cabin who always wore leggings and a messy top bun. Quiet, inscrutable Ellie held up her piece of paper to reveal a crudely drawn figure with dots for eyes and a circle for a mouth that looked a little like Shrek. Amelia's was the most accurate. *OK, but that's not as hard*, said Morgan, since Amelia's body didn't have the same convexities and folds that some of ours did. Skinny bodies are all more or less the same, but at camp, I'd become intimately acquainted with all the ways a person could be fat. My calves were eerily slender for my body size, but one girl in the fourteen-to-sixteen-year-old division had enormous ones that were almost as wide as her thighs. My fat lived mostly in my middle, but some girls were widest at the top, like opera singers, and others had giant asses, and the asses could be different too, some rounder at the top, some squarish, others onion shaped. I learned that hips could fall in different places—I carried mine high, next to my stomach, but others carried theirs low. Some girls, like me, had pillowy chins and cheeks, while others maintained an uncanny angularity. The boys, who we saw much less of, had different bodies too. Some had breasts and some didn't. Some had thick thighs and some had pin legs.

The mirror has long been the symbol of negative self-image, and fat teenage girls were said to fear it. But mirrors were never my problem. Your reflected body still belongs to you. Alone in a quiet room, it's yours to bend and contort and twist. When you dart out of frame, it goes with you. Pictures were what terrified me. Whenever Charlie or Morgan tried to take one with their digital cameras, I fled. Pictures told you the truth, which is to say, they showed you as everyone else saw you. You on the news, you on the magazine cover, as a before, as an after. My photographed body was more real than the one in the mirror because it was the one that didn't belong to me at all.

That night, the Super Seniors and a few counselors sat in J-14. Charlie and Morgan were splayed across Charlie's bunk. I sat next to Amelia on mine, and Dede sat near our feet. McKenna, one of the skinny girls, had taken a second shower after the evening activity, and joined us as she towel dried her hair. *I wish I had your body*, Dede sighed. A size 6 at most, McKenna had gotten used to being the reflecting pool for our self-loathing. She accepted her role about as graciously as she could—by reminding us that she hated herself just as much. *Well, my ass looks like two potatoes fighting in a bag,* she offered.

I wonder what it's like to lose all your weight, said Dede (at camp, weight took a possessive pronoun). *I did it,* said Kristy. We jerked our heads toward her. Knowing that our counselor had once been in our world and had crossed over, that her body wasn't a thing she took for granted but a hard-won gift, this made her a thing of awe. It was as if she'd seen the afterlife. We all started speaking at once—how did she do it, were people nicer, how did she do it, could she shop anywhere, how did she do it, did guys talk to her more, how did she do it, could we do it too? She answered dutifully. Yes, people were nicer. Yes, guys talked to her more. Yes, she could shop at regular stores now. *Can you feel it?* asked Dede. Always, this was what we wanted to know—how it *felt* to be thin, the physical reality of it. Most of us had never experienced thinness. If you want to know what it feels like to be taller, or shorter, or fatter, you can hunch, or get a step stool, or put on a fat suit, you can add or subtract certain things to, if only crudely, approximate the world from this new perspective. But you can't warp into a thinner body, not even temporarily, and so when we imagined living as thin people, it was not our bodies, shrunken, but the laws of physics, rewritten. We always had questions for the thin girls at camp: *Do you feel heavy when you sit down? Does your stomach fold or is it like nothing? Do your thighs spread out? Do your pants leave dents?* Kristy had defied the laws of fatness and entered the realm of the thin. Could she feel it? *I don't know, I still have these,* she held out her arms, shook them, and looked down into her lap as we

erupted in a chorus of *No you look SO good* and *I'm so jealous.*
When she looked up, there were tears in her eyes. *I'm never
gonna know what I look like,* she said quietly.

———

As my mom filled out forms before camp started, she came
across one about an optional trip to a water park. She turned her
desk chair to face me and asked if I wanted to go. I said, without
hesitation, absolutely not. I used to love the water. On vacations
I'd swim in the pool for hours, staying submerged so long that
my dad would leave, then my mom, then my brothers, until it
was just me careening back and forth from the shallow end to
the deep while my grandma looked on, patient in a way I still
don't understand. I jumped into an outdoor hotel pool in Wisconsin in November because I missed it so much. The hate I felt
toward my pudgy little tube body was somehow suspended in
the water, so I didn't care who saw me in a bathing suit.

Until high school. Suddenly, the idea became intolerable.
My boarding school had a brand-new world-class pool that my
best friend would visit a few times a week. I lied and told her
I couldn't swim.

Most of the campers had signed up for the water-park trip,
so when the day came and all the yellow school buses had
pulled out of the dusty parking lot, it was just me and a few
other Super Seniors with nothing to do. Our days were usually
packed with activity, but today, we had hours to fill. Someone suggested sunbathing. I'd never sunbathed before. But I
followed Charlie, Alana, Ellie, and Amelia out to a patch of
grass that lay overlooking the big hill. Charlie wore an oversize

T-shirt over spandex shorts. Ellie wore the big basketball shorts she always wore. Alana stripped down to a bikini. I eyed her flat stomach.

Save for a few run-ins with other kids, nobody outside my family ever said anything bad about my body. Still, I knew it was a problem, and I was constantly tense with the knowledge. In first grade, I began to suck in my stomach, first in the mirror, then in public, then all the time, and from there I never stopped. I still do it now, not by choice, but because it's become the central tension around which my body orients its movements. It is a second spine. If I try to let my stomach out while I'm standing up, I don't know how to breathe properly. Around the same time I started sucking in, I started squeezing my butt cheeks together to take up less space, which I've realized recently only makes my ass appear strange and squashed, like Hank Hill's. When I was twenty-five and in my first relationship, I began to let someone see my body clearly. Kylie looked at me from the bed and asked me to try and let my ass hang free, and I stood there trying, leaning on the dresser and willing my muscles to release, but I couldn't. I only knew how to clench.

The five of us splayed out on the grass. I shook my towel flat and sat down in my Soffe shorts, quietly rolling the sleeves of my T-shirt up to even out my farmer tan. This was something. Even in the sticky July of camp, I would not wear tank tops. Nobody said much. For weeks we'd all spent every minute together, panting beside one another in aerobics, peeing in adjacent stalls, shaving our legs side by side on the porch with a cup of water, saying good night in our parallel beds, and I could feel it all settling over us now, the kind of intimacy that is earned through wordless proximity. Charlie lifted her shirt a little to wipe sweat off her forehead. I did the same. Then she rolled the shirt up a few inches and tucked it under the band of her sports bra. I did too. My belly was smooth and white like a fish. I touched it self-consciously, so much paler and softer than any other part of my body. Charlie flipped over onto her stomach and propped her head up in her hands. I did too. I gazed down the hill to the pool, which overlooked the glittering lake, the other side of it thicketed with pines and oaks. It was rumored that the campsite hosted a nudist retreat for gay men every September, shortly after fat camp ended. I also knew, from googling, that the camp had hosted a lesbian retreat in the fall of 1988 where there was chanting, drumbeating, dancing, and more nudity. I imagined these people, the men and the women, sprawled out naked on deck chairs, on towels along the sandy shore, the meat of their thighs, stomachs, breasts, tensing and jiggling as they panted up the hill to the mess hall, as they danced together in the rec hall, as they lay together in their bunks. I imagined body hair and mingled limbs. I wondered if I'd ever be able to feel like that. With my bare back to the sun, I laid my head on my arms and fell asleep.

The next morning, when I woke up and rolled over in my bunk, I felt a stinging pain. I walked over to the bathroom and looked in the mirror. Above my ass was an angry red mountain range. Having never bared it in public before, I'd forgotten that my back, like the rest of my body, was prone to burning. I winced as I put on my T-shirt to walk to breakfast, and as I sweated through aerobics, the beads of saltwater stung like droplets on a hot pan.

During free period, we sat on the same hill we had the day before. Rebecca, a Super Senior from the other cabin, brought a guitar. Rebecca was from New Jersey, had chin-length red hair, always dressed in baggy shorts and tall tees. Rebecca was jocular, self-effacing, endearingly boyish, and though Rebecca's queerness only vaguely registered to me then, and my own even less so, what I did know was that I wanted very deeply for Rebecca to think I was cool. As I lay down on the grass, Amelia noticed my grimace and asked what was wrong. I said it was all right, just a little burn. She asked if she could see, and with reluctance, I lifted my shirt slightly to show her. *Ouch*, she said, and before I could assure her that it was really OK, she was jogging up the hill, calling behind her, *Gonna go get some aloe from Bob.*

Several minutes later, Amelia came back down cupping a heap of single-use aloe packets. Instead of handing them to me as I expected she would, she ripped one open and squeezed the goo onto her finger. *Here*, she said, motioning for me to turn around. I was mildly stunned. It would never have occurred to me to outsource this task. Even though I'd lived in dorms at boarding school, played team sports, had best friends, found kinship and safety in girls all my life, I let nobody but doctors touch me. But here was Amelia rubbing aloe onto my bare skin, her movements careful, but light with the nonchalance of someone for whom this was no big deal. Maybe it could be this easy. After she was done, I thanked her and closed my eyes. Rebecca had begun to strum a song I'd never heard before. It was a love song, the kind that's filled with the words *whoa* and *hey hey*, and the word *love*, which is deployed liberally and

without any bashfulness. I listened to love songs all the time,
but they were not sweet or soft in this way. My music taste
was one of the few cool things I had to offer, so I gripped it
tightly to my chest. Usually, the love songs I fell asleep listening to had some kind of discordant element, whether a heavy
distortion pedal or tortured unmet longing. Hearing this song
at this moment from Rebecca, whose bravado had suddenly
dissolved into blushing earnestness, I wanted to hear it fifty
more times. I was too nervous to ask the name of the song,
but I made a mental note of some of the lyrics—*I won't hesi-
tate, look into your heart, the sky is yours*—and muttered them to
myself over and over again through dinner (turkey meatloaf)
and evening activity (cheer night) so I wouldn't forget them.
By the time I finally got back to the cabin, the muttering had
become incantatory, the jumble of phrases engraved into my
mouth by muscle memory. No longer did I have to will myself
to repeat the words. They looped forward on their own with
the propulsiveness of chant, of prayer. When it was finally lights
out, I turned to Morgan and tapped her on the shoulder. She
used the browser on her contraband flip phone to look up the
lyrics for me. *It says it's by Jason Mraz,* she said, and I fell asleep.

By the end of camp, I'd lost twenty-five pounds. Charlie
lost thirty-six. Some girls lost forty, fifty. It became real only
when we saw our parents' mouths hang open in surprise. *Wow*
was followed by *You look so different* and then *How do you feel?*
We'd asked ourselves this question for weeks, years, only to
realize that the answer would always exist outside of us. We
could say we perspired a little less, chafed a little less, that
waistbands and chairs cut into us less, or differently, but we

couldn't lie still in our darkened beds and summon a feeling of difference.

As the sun set each night, we would head together up the hill to dinner, luxuriating in the feeling of being clean and warm and damp, our muscles exhausted but loose with the pleasure of it, our hair curling at the nape and lightly perfumed with apple-scented shampoo. As I fell asleep, I'd idly stroke my stomach or my upper arm, squeezing the fat gently like a fruit I'd just picked. In the dark like that, it felt lush, supple, a type of silk you could eat. According to camp lore, your fat would feel squishiest right before it disappeared, and so we touched our own bodies tenderly, searchingly, hoping, for the first and only time, to find softness.

Storm Lake, Part 2

SHE ARRIVED IN ILLINOIS WITH one suitcase filled with clothes and two garbage bags filled with brochures, gum wrappers, financial documents, mail, and several dozen warm letters of farewell from her elementary and middle school students. She repeated the same three sentences over and over again. *I taught for thirty-eight and a half years*, she said, always including the fraction, *and I'm proud of that. But now* . . . Her eyes trailed past me and toward an invisible ship on the horizon, *I'm ready to be unknown.* At the time, the wish confused me: she was one of the friendliest people I'd ever met. But in the fifteen years since, she mostly kept her promise. She knew Richard, a retired day-trader neighbor who'd never married, who helped her with her lawn sometimes. She knew Linda, a neighbor who sold tchotchkes on eBay and sometimes drove her to appointments. She took an annual phone call with her sister, went to Arizona once to visit her childhood best friend, but otherwise, she was happy to be alone.

Except she wasn't alone, not entirely at least. We saw her all the time: on the weekends, on vacations, when she babysat, and in the several-month period where she lived in our basement. I loved it. The only person who complained about her presence was the person who continued to invite her. In the picture my dad painted of his mother, she was wicked, neglectful, a cartoon. But if anyone was wicked, it seemed to me, it was him. She told me that they'd never gotten along, that she couldn't figure out how she'd raised such a person, and I couldn't either. He seemed needlessly mean to her, mocking her pride for teaching, the way she used midwestern phrases like *Jeepers Christmas*, the junior college she attended, how much she liked to talk to strangers. He was full of hubris, but he was never proud of anyone. He didn't hug, didn't soothe, didn't encourage. He was tense and angry, screaming at us for dropping a fork or a cup at dinner, terrifying if our voices from downstairs interrupted his conference call. His principal role as a parent was money and its enforcement.

A lot of our fights were about what he called *work*. Work wasn't housework, like dishes and cleaning up after the dog. Most of that work was left to my mom. Work was the weekends he decided to rearrange his piles, to move the dining room table's mess up to the attic, or to clear out the attic and write down each item before we gave it all to Goodwill. Work was carrying Bankers Boxes up and down the stairs. Work was hours in the stuffy storage units, in our airless carless garage among tangled piles of metal and plastic that reached near to the ceiling. My older brothers worked without complaint, and so they were good. But I often refused, because it was tedious, because I didn't like him, because I'd rather watch TV, because the table and the attic would always fill up again anyway. I didn't work. And so I was bad.

Once, in a fight about work, he yelled that I was a *goddamn lazy sack of shit*. The next day, after I had cried about it alone in my room, the phrase seemed absurd, lifted out of a Lifetime movie. It became a running private joke between me and my middle school best friend, *GLSOS*, not something that made us laugh, necessarily, but an oddity we took out occasionally to marvel at. Its cruelty was cartoonish. *You fight with him for the same reason I did*, my grandma said once. *You're too similar*. I didn't agree. She and I loved each other. We were nothing like him.

Grandma moved out of the basement when she bought her condo. In the early days when it contained only furniture, a glass bowl filled with colored stones, and a smattering of dishes and silverware, she'd allow all of us in. After a year, only my younger brother and I could enter, and by the second year, her door was sealed. We used to pick her up every Sunday to go to Costco. My brother rang the bell, then she'd open the door a crack and slip out, a plastic grocery bag clutched in her hand. The contents of the bag always seemed random, papers and wrappers, as if she'd dipped it down into the house like a bucket before lifting it, and locking up the rest.

She made one attempt to return to Storm Lake. She booked a flight and packed a bag. Her friend Paula was going to pick her up from the airport in Omaha and drive her the two and a half hours east. She seemed nervous but excited to visit her old friends, her old school, her old house. On the day she was set to fly back to Storm Lake, a 747 smashed into the World Trade Center. Her plane never left O'Hare. For months, she was too scared to fly, and she postponed the trip for when she wasn't scared anymore. She had time to wait, and the house wasn't going anywhere. But as one fear began to dissipate, another slid into its place. The house wasn't going anywhere. She had time to wait. After that, there was no talk of going back.

═══

When I was eighteen, I moved to Iowa for college, and when I was twenty-three, I moved back again for graduate school. In these years, I was only ever a few hours from Storm Lake, and always aware of this fact. When anyone asked why I chose to go to school in Iowa, I didn't know what to say. *My dad's family is from there*, I offered. If I met a born-and-bred Iowan, I asked them if they knew my grandma's town, and if I saw someone wearing a shirt with the state's name, I pointed to it and said, to whoever I was with, *Iowa*. Storm Lake felt like my claim to the state, or my claim to some kind of family legacy. Though I could barely picture the place, it was a landmark. In my senior year of college, I gained access to a car, and suddenly the whole of Iowa opened up before me. I toyed with the idea of a visit, but every time I considered spending a weekend in Storm Lake, something more pressing would come up, a research paper or a hangover or another party in a dirt basement. Storm Lake intrigued me, but my curiosity was never urgent. It still wasn't going anywhere.

Neither was my grandmother. Nearing ninety and very much alive, she spent much of her time going or preparing to go to doctors' appointments, which for her was as much a pleasant diversion as it was a medical necessity. For her age, she'd remained remarkably healthy, but she came to relish the ritual of care. When I drove her into Chicago once for a psychiatrist's appointment, she came out not with insight or understanding but with stories about her doctor. *He refilled my Lithium*, she said, *but really, we just visited*. Afterward, we went to a Jamba Juice near her house, and the manager came out from behind the counter to give her a hug. The same thing happened at Panera Bread, where I learned that my grandma had given her favorite cashier money for college textbooks. Grandma told me the life stories of her massage therapist, her mailman, the manager at a different, unrelated juice store. Being adored by strangers, I realized, was her preferred way to remain unknown.

The rest of her time she spent on the internet. Somehow, she had figured out Facebook, and it quickly became her principal life force. From her laptop she shared several dozen articles and memes a day, each promoting a lifestyle I'd never known her to value. She did not sew, did not cook, had never prided herself on keeping house or being a mother, and had long ago renounced her Catholic faith, but her feed suggested otherwise. There were tips for living: *8 Simple Recipes for Your Paleo Life* and *How to Raise Your Personal Energy Vibrations* and *How to Cherish the Little Moments with Your Children* and *12 Household Items to Make Your Home Sparkle*. There were recipes for skull-shaped Halloween pizza pockets, cheesy scalloped potatoes, Crockpot taco lasagna, eggnog French toast. A photo of a beach said *Wish I was five coconut rum drinks deep in the Bahamas*. A photo of Winnie the Pooh said *Today, let's just choose to be happy*. There were butterflies that said *Good Night My Friends, I pray that God's angels stand guard over you*, a menorah that said *Happy Hanukkah*, a tree that said *The greatest Christmas gift is being with your family*. Another post said *Yes, I do depend on a man. He depends on me and I depend on him. That's*

how marriage is supposed to work. She'd told me she regretted
every day of her marriage. She hadn't come to Christmas in
years. Some shares seemed untethered to any sense of social
performance or self-identification, had no imperative, no wisdom. Once, she shared the website for Home Depot (*I invest
in their stock*, she explained to me). Another time, the privacy
policy for the *Daily Mail* (*I thought it was good for people to have*).
Some posts remained inexplicable, like the one that simply said
BIG POT OF CHILI: YAY OR NAY?

Many of her Facebook shares were from a group called
I Grew Up in Iowa! The group was filled with questions of
memory. *Who remembers baling hay? Who remembers the ding ding
sound when you pulled into a full-service gas station? Does anyone remember the name of the lime pits on the south of the Salis-
bury house? The place in Derby where the old gals served family-style
meals? The crooked bridge between Muscatine and Illinois? Who here
has heard of my hometown Wadena, Who here has heard of my hometown Volga, Does anyone know what kind of worm this is?*

The group's urgent call to memory was perhaps a correc-
tive to the fact that Iowa isn't much remembered by the people
outside it. When I was growing up, if my dad was talking about
Iowa, he was making fun of it. He said it was an acronym for
Idiots Out Walking Around. When other people talked about it,
they were usually searching for an example of a far-flung place,
not exotic and across the world like Timbuktu, but domesti-
cally remote, a familiar type of alien, a place nobody comes
from or goes to but that everyone can picture. Even the name
sounded weird, mushy and consonantless. It made your mouth
just hang open.

Before she was my grandma, she was Peggy, born in Albert City, Iowa, in 1935, and she never took to her name. Her younger sister is Jo, and she never took to her either, but that's not quite how she phrases it. She sighs, instead, *Me and Jo are different*, or *She was always the outgoing one*, or *Dad liked her because she liked sports*. They grew up on a farm, where her mother raised hens and her father raised everything else. The first thing anyone remembers about her father is that he was short—barely cleared five feet. The second is that he was personable. The third is that he drank. People for whom farms are holiday attractions, not livelihoods—people like me—tend to assume that everyone who farms must be very good at it, a kind of romantic, salt-of-the-earth calling, but lots, like her dad, just sort of inherit them like an ill-fitting coat. He was all right enough at it. Her mother was small too, barely a hundred pounds and reserved, but virtuosic with the hens. She fussed over them like children, constantly adjusting the temperature of the coop, the composition of their feed. She sang lullabies to them, and in turn, they laid the county's best eggs. Sometimes, Grandma would talk about helping her mother with the chickens and still, seventy years later, she told it like a war story. The smell, the noise, the flashes of feathered wing. All her life, she has never been able to stomach poultry. Instead, she orders steak, well done.

When she was about to turn twenty-three, as she approached the age at which hesitation would calcify into identity, she found a husband. Len was a quiet man who'd dropped out of college but worked his way up to buying the

oil jobbership and service station where his own father had
worked. Len bought oil and diesel from a company, distrib-
uted it, and leased the station to another person, who managed
it. Compared to Len's family, Peggy's was relatively well-off.
They made enough money that her parents could send her to
a junior college, enough money that her wedding announcement in the *Storm Lake Pilot-Tribune* mentioned a queen's
crown of seed pearls and a reception at the Cobblestone Inn.
The paper noted everything, from Peggy's fingertip veil to her
simple button earrings to the pearl prayer book given to her by
the bridegroom. It named the cousins who served as acolytes,
the friends and family members who organized the gift table
and coordinated the buffet lunch. On the table were horns of
plenty filled with her chosen colors: rust, dark green, and gold.
The passage was longer than an obituary, and at the end, it
listed the couple's street address. This was a small-town newspaper. This was everyone's life. Later, the paper would report
when Len got a permit to build a wood garage on his parents' property and when someone took his tan car coat at the
Knights of Columbus meeting. They ran a story when Peggy
was out sick with the flu and when Len went to the hospital
for diabetic shock (he'd had type 1 since he was a child). It
advertised the station's grand opening, where lollipops were
handed out by Octane the Clown. Each time one of Peggy's
friends had gotten married, which they'd done steadily ever
since graduating from high school, the paper had announced
that too. It noted her presence at every last one, manning the
coffee station, clutching red roses.

Her marriage voided her teaching contract. It was 1957

and it was school board policy. The logic was threefold: First, it ensured that rural towns could receive a steady stream of young, educated women who would rotate into the school system, meet and marry one of the town's bachelors, and then rotate out, making room for the next girl. Second, married women shouldn't need a second income. Third, a married woman would soon become a mother, and teaching might split her reserves of love and nurture in half, or worse, asymmetrically. But she began to miss teaching desperately. She wondered, had wondered ever since she got engaged, if it had been worth giving up. She convinced the school board to let her work part-time until her son went to pre-K, and when the district finally reversed their policy, she threw herself back in full-time.

To call teaching rewarding would be a cliché if it didn't describe, precisely, the gratification it gave her. We consider a job rewarding when its social value far outstrips its pay. Hedge fund managers are rewarded handsomely, so they'd never use the word. Indeed, teaching barely paid a livable salary. But her husband made decent money, and she'd one day inherit the family farm, and she was so frugal, anyway, that she didn't need much to live on. Teaching was rewarding because its emotional inputs felt, unlike marriage, unlike motherhood, proportionate to their outputs. To be responsible for a child's education was a precious task, but her role in their enrichment was so singular, so crystalline, that the government paid her to do it. She showed up and the kids showed up at the same time every day. She spoke and they listened. Her job was to teach them to read. They began to sound out letters until the letters became words and the words became sentences. She watched the world cohere before their eyes and marked their dawning awareness with stickers, letters, numbers. They drew her pictures and wrote her cards and still, decades later, will find her on Facebook to thank her. Being on the clock was not suffocating, to her. It was, in fact, the only type of time that did not feel interminable, each relationship punctuated by bells, recesses, breaks, relief. She loved her students. She loved that every day they went back to their houses. She loved the twenty-minute drive between school and home when time clicked shut for a moment and she could luxuriate in the space between the something she'd just done and everything she had left to do.

Iowa is filled with some of the richest soil in the world. That vast expanse of farmland is divided into thousands of one-mile-by-one-mile squares. Those squares are then split into four parcels of land. For decades, each parcel contained one farm and one family who cultivated it. The farms produced modest yields and made modest money, and the government helped ensure this modesty by floating farmers when yield dipped low, stabilizing prices when yield soared. I have a memory of visiting the family farm as a child. An adult gripped my armpits and lowered me barefoot onto a long, tilled mound of soil. Immediately, my feet sank in. It was wet, not like the greedy suction of wet sand, nor the shallow anemic squish of backyard dirt after rain. It was moist, a lush word hated only by people who feel alienated from their own bodily functions. It was like no material I'd ever stepped in, pillowed and pliable and a little sticky, like butter cake. I was stepping in freshly plowed topsoil, soft and sensuous as a pile of shit, which it fractionally was, and I didn't care a bit. It felt incredible.

Iowa is also filled with hogs. And cows. And sheep. Many

Iowa towns have long been ruled by their meatpacking facilities. When my dad was a child in Storm Lake, it was the
Hygrade pork plant. Hygrade employed six hundred people,
making it by far the biggest employer in town. All day, the
workers at Hygrade slaughtered hogs and cleaved them into
huge, red hunks. *There's no good, pleasant jobs in the packing plant*,
a former supervisor once said in an interview, *but when the pay-
checks came around, it made it worthwhile*. Hygrade was a union
plant, which meant good wages, health insurance, and pensions,
which meant that workers often stayed in the job for decades.
Many of my dad's classmates came from meatpacking families, and on these salaries, which could easily hit six figures in
today's dollars, it was possible to own a boat, an RV, *and* a house
of your own. The plant granted entry into the middle class.

———

Growing up, my dad assumed his family was poor. That they
had a house, two cars, and a business in town, these facts felt
immaterial to a child. Poverty was the only way to explain his
mother's refusal to spend money on things other kids got. His
existence, it seemed, was bleeding her dry. She didn't buy him
the toys he wanted. She complained constantly about the cost
of his clothes and school supplies. When she agreed to pay the
five dollars for Little League registration, she refused to buy the
glove. Coach Bob, who lived across the street, inquired with
confusion about why the family couldn't get him one. The
couple owned a ranch home, just like Bob did. They perched
comfortably within the middle class, just like Bob did. They
grudgingly got my dad the cheapest glove they could find.

This version of my grandma sounded cartoonish in his sto-ries. Again and again, she denied him what she could easily pro-vide. Sometimes, the stories Dad told to illustrate neglect seemed almost comically woebegone, like a fable about orphans that somehow always involved sports equipment. When he needed track shoes, he had to borrow an old pair from Jeff Judson. When he wanted Chuck Taylors like everybody else on his bas-ketball team, he had to fish a ratty pair out of the trash and cover the holes with green Sharpie. In second grade, he signed up for free lunch and extra milk, thinking he qualified. In fifth grade, as part of the free-lunch agreement—an indenture banned now but legal then—he started working in the cafeteria. In seventh grade, finally of legal age, he started working in the meat room at SuperValu, carefully wiping down the cleavers and industrial slicing machines. From then on, he always had a job. He thought he was relieving his parents of a burden, but more and more, the adults around him seemed confused by his parents' frugality. Bob seemed confused. Jeff Judson's mother seemed confused. His own grandparents seemed confused—in fact they seemed *angry*—and by the time the school administrators noticed his inclusion on the free-lunch list, put two and two together, and gently informed him that they'd have to take him off, he realized his family wasn't poor at all. But if poverty didn't explain their burden, what did? However much money his parents had in their coffers, from then on, he knew not to rely on it. Generosity was fickle, so he would continue to rely on the one thing that had never denied him, the only relationship whose debts were enforceable. Work, he would always have work.

It was his grandparents who eventually bought him new

shoes and a better glove. His grandparents who took him to practices and recitals, who drove him around the neighborhood to finish his paper route if it was snowing, who hung his laundry out on the backyard line to dry. In the story of his childhood, their house countered the disorder of his own. His grandfather was calm and quiet. His grandmother was fierce and neat. After school, instead of returning home, he often went to theirs, where his grandmother made him a scrambled egg sandwich. When his own mother came home from school, she changed into her nightie, either oblivious to his presence or hoping to will it away, and sat down to eat a tin of beans at the kitchen table. On Friday afternoons, she went straight from the front door to her bed. She'd stay there the whole weekend if she could.

When his acceptance letter from the Ivy League arrived in the mail, he didn't bother asking who would pay. He deferred his enrollment and joined the army. When he got back from basic training, he became the night manager at the SuperValu and detasseled corn on the side. After a year, he'd saved up enough for his first two semesters—unfathomable now but possible then—and he drove his '64 Oldsmobile to New Haven to begin his first year. In the summers, he worked hundred-hour weeks and made good union money fixing air conditioners for GE. Loans covered the rest.

It was the tail end of the '70s, and agriculture in Iowa didn't look the same as it had in the '60s. Back then, meat plants operated by slaughtering the animals and hacking them into quarters or halves, which were shipped in trucks to grocery stores. There, skilled butchers were the ones to carefully dissect the massive hunks into the cuts people bought and ate.

But in the late '60s, a company called Iowa Beef Packers found a much more efficient way to pack meat. IBP's system turned one skilled, high-paid butcher into dozens of workers standing shoulder to shoulder on a freezing disassembly line. As each carcass rolled through, one worker made his prescribed cut, then the next made his, the meat rolling down the belt until it was a heap of vacuum-packed chunks. These were placed in a box and arrived at the grocery store ready to be bought, faster and cheaper than ever before, no butcher needed. *We've tried to take the skill out of every step*, IBP had explained. Their beef plants began springing up in rural towns across the country.

As the old way of meatpacking began to look inefficient, so too did the old way of farming: too many workers for too little yield, too many subsidies for too little profit. Nixon's secretary of agriculture encouraged farmers to go big, bigger, to go big or get out, and so they bought more land and planted more crops, fencerow to fencerow. The plan worked: farming became more prosperous than ever before. Where farming was once, at most, a modest vocation, it now dangled the possibility of making you rich. Peggy's parents were too old to farm by then, and so they moved to an apartment in town, leasing their land to a family they'd known for years. They made fine money before the boom, and they didn't need more now, so they didn't buy in. But all across Iowa, all across the Midwest, many other farmers followed the glint in the distance.

At the start of my dad's junior year of college, he ran out of money. This was not his plan. He had always paid his own way, but the financial aid office noticed that his parents, on paper at least, had the means to share his burden. He told the school his situation: his parents had their money, and he had his. But the school didn't believe him—most parents winced at the bill, yes, but few outright refused to pay it. The school revoked his loans, and he was asked to leave the dorms. In September, he drove the Oldsmobile twenty hours across Pennsylvania, Ohio, Indiana, Illinois, through the wavy part of Iowa until it was flat and almost Nebraska, back to his parents, back to Storm Lake, his hometown, which was about to change forever.

Dad needed $10,000 to get back to college, and he resented having to ask for help. But at a minimum-wage job, it would take a person a year and a half to earn that much money. Even at Hygrade, it would've taken six months. If he wanted to get back for the spring semester, he'd need to earn it in three. With his parents, he struck up an agreement: if he did all the work they asked him to do, they'd pay his way back to college. And so he spent that fall doing everything they asked. He built them a new patio in the backyard. He installed an automatic garage door opener. He helped out at the station. He pulled weeds and mowed the lawn like he had as a kid.

That October, Hygrade closed the Storm Lake meat processing plant. Over the last decade, IBP and its boxed beef had come to rule the industry, and now, they'd set their sights on pork. To compete with IBP's margins, Hygrade began asking workers to do more work for less money, ramping up production while threatening to slash pay. The union held them off for a few years, until Hygrade announced that it had decided to shut the whole plant down. Storm Lake lost its biggest employer, and six hundred men were out of a job. Across the Midwest, more meat plants were closing. The farmers weren't faring much better. The land that had been valuable during the boom was losing its value, and inflation and interest rates were climbing. The whole state was worried about what lay ahead.

In December, my dad sat with his parents at the breakfast table. His mom was reading the paper, front to back as she always did. The front page declared SORE SPOTS NOTED IN LOCAL ECONOMY. St. Paul's Lutheran Church was having a celebratory mortgage burning. KFC advertised a holiday special, and the Accidents section announced that a snowball had broken a school bus window. When she got to the back of the issue, in the Legal section, her face went ashen. Printed there, under the names of her husband and his business partner Ernie, was a judgment of debt from the bank. Ernie and Len owed $26,000. Len told her that it was because Ernie had simply been lenient and let too many people buy gas on credit. He said he hadn't known how to break the news to her so he'd simply decided to lie, and here, in the newspaper, was how she had to find out. Her son tried to calm her down, suggesting that they could make up the difference, that they could write it off as a business loss. Her husband insisted he'd sort it all out. What did they know, she thought. She'd gripped her money so tightly for so long, let it form a nest around the life she'd never even wanted, and here she was, sitting before the two men who'd tethered her life to theirs as they insisted that money was not such a big deal. That night, she moved her things to the spare room. At Christmas, she barely spoke to her husband. *I never should have trusted him*, she told me later. *And I never did again.*

A few weeks after Christmas, she accompanied my dad to the bank. He stood beside her at the counter and made conversation with the teller, who was a girl he'd gone to school with. He'd been working the past few months, he explained, and they were there to withdraw his payment. For three months, he'd done everything his parents had asked. He expected his mother to ask the teller to withdraw the $10,000 she had promised him. To the teller, his mom said *$400*. He looked at his mom's face for some kind of acknowledgment, an awareness that the verbal contract between them had been breached. He imagined that, if he looked long enough, he'd find a brain inside her brain with which he could exchange glances, a brain that, even if it couldn't stop her breaking her promise, could at least recognize the fact of the breaking. But she looked past him and the teller, straight ahead at the clock. That night, he got in the Oldsmobile and drove back the way he came. It was January 1982.

In this new decade, the prosperity of the '70s wasn't sticking. Over the next few years, this downturn would become a crisis. As farmers' loans defaulted and their livelihoods went into free fall, the government that previously encouraged them did nothing. The same people who'd been celebrated for feeding the country now found themselves at food banks. Many farmers protested, thousands of them, driving their tractors down the streets of Washington, gathering at foreclosure auctions and chanting *No sale* as their neighbors lost their land. Some hanged themselves in their barns. Others left the state. By the end of the decade, a quarter of the farms had closed, taking with them banks, small businesses, entire Main Streets.

Meanwhile, the Hygrade plant reopened after only a year, but this time, under new ownership: IBP. Some of the former Hygrade workers applied for their old jobs, but IBP didn't want anyone who remembered how things had been before. Instead, they filled the plant with workers from outside Storm Lake. At first, these new workers came from surrounding towns, then from surrounding states, and, finally, from other countries. In the mid-'80s came Laotian families who'd been made refugees by the Vietnam War. In the early '90s came workers whom IBP had recruited from Mexico. Their pay was less than half what the Hygrade employees had made, and their work twice as dangerous. By the time my grandma left Storm Lake in 2000, people from these two groups made up half the town's population and most of the plant's workforce. Rural towns across the Midwest got scooped out by the farm crisis, and many never fully recovered. Storm Lake looked very different than it had twenty years earlier, but it was not dead.

———

By the time I moved back to Iowa for grad school, nobody in my family had seen my grandma for years. She wasn't bedbound or housebound in any way. She was mad.

She was mad at Justin Trudeau.

IN MY OPINION, SOME PEOPLE CANNOT HANDLE
ACCESS TO THE PUBLIC PURSESTRINGS. THANK GOD
MY PARENTS TAUGHT ME TO SPEND OTHER'S MONEY AS
I WOULD SPEND MY OWN.

She was mad at Madonna.

> "HOLLYWOOD TYPES" PREFER LEMMINGS NOT
> THINKERS! MOST ARE JUST TRYING TO INFLUENCE THE
> MASSES THAT ARE GULLIBLE ENOUGH TO LISTEN TO
> THEM. THEY LIVE IN AN INSULAR WORLD—DO-NOT-BE-
> FOOLED-BY-THEIR-AUDACITY!!!!!

She was mad at a salad recipe.

> ONLY QUESTION PRESERVATIVES IN BACON?

She was mad at a third-tier acquaintance that none of us, including her, had ever met.

> I CAN SEE WHY YOUR CLASSES ARE SOOO SMALL AND
> YOURE AN ADJUNCT PROFESSOR.
>
> *Hey Peggy the world isn't your corner of Iowa. And take off
> the all caps.*

When someone intervened to ask what happened, she said
only this:

> HE CALLED ME A HAYSEED.

Above all, she was mad at her son. They hadn't said a word
to each other in seven years, and it was unclear if they ever
would again. They aimed their anger at money.

When my mom's father died and his will was read, it was revealed that the sums he'd bequeathed to each of his children were not equal, but differentiated by income. It divided the family, or really, it simply reinscribed divisions that existed long before money was involved. Never mind that the long-suspected inequities of love that the money supposedly confirmed were misaligned with the actual brackets into which each child had been slotted. The son who got the most was not his father's favorite, but in fact the child he'd been cruelest to, while the most dutiful child had received a middling amount, and the two who got the least had never faced any extreme of adoration or scorn. If the sums of money were evidence of anything besides need, it was not approval, nor love. It was guilt. But my own dad became obsessed with the injustice of it all. He spent car rides and dinners dissecting it over and over again. He brought it up at weddings and funerals. He almost skipped my high school graduation because one of the aunts who got more would be there. My dad cared about the money far more than my mom did, cared about it until her pain became his own. He gnawed on it, guarded it, jealously, like a bone.

In his own mother's will was a legacy he could perfect. He saw a way to make things whole. Peggy had been middle class her whole life but, in her old age, had finally become rich through pathological frugality, a complex and boring series of investments and mutual funds and something called IPERS, and finally, the simple fact that she had stubbornly managed to outlive a lot of people, except, of course, her only son. Immediately, they clashed. He wanted her to die having already funneled to her heirs as many untaxable assets as she legally could.

She wanted to die with a big number by her name. He thought she ought to move her money around, maximize its value. She thought he was robbing her and calling her stupid. First, she stopped coming to dinner every week, then she stopped coming to Thanksgiving, then they stopped emailing, then she announced that she'd met with an estate lawyer. She was ending his inheritance and revoking his share in the family farm. The money wasn't going far—she was rerouting it to us, his children, which is exactly what he'd have done upon receiving it too. Otherwise, the money would've sat in his bank account the same way it sat in hers, because neither of them had a use for it: she was so frugal that she wouldn't even buy herself a third pair of comfy slacks, and he was so rich that his desires could never outrun his assets. Her will had no material consequence. But it was freighted with loathing, and the architecture of loathing was robust; the architecture of capital proved so tempting a toehold.

———

Because they refused to communicate, they spoke indirectly through me, always by email, my family's favorite medium. His were brief and terse. Birthdays got two words, *Happy birthday*, then a period, then his email signature, which included a legal disclaimer many times longer than the message itself. Her emails were sprawling, sparsely punctuated, and always in all caps, not, as I'd assumed, to communicate anger or fervor, but because, as she told me, the big letters were easier for her to see. She always used the subject line *In Touch*, because if she didn't put a subject, Gmail would ask her if she was sure she wanted to leave it blank. She was never sure.

We three were like middle school crushes in the hallway. When I asked her to come to Thanksgiving dinner one year, both she and my dad exploded. It was unclear what exactly they were protesting. She rejected my invitation by insisting that she wasn't invited. He forbade her from attending by complaining that she'd refused to come. Their anger was a math problem whose like terms could be reduced and reduced until one side equaled the other.

I DID NOT CREATE THIS SITUATION. MY SON HAS BEEN A PAIN IN THE ASS FOR YEARS.

I see she is back to all caps. Hopefully, for her own sake, she will die soon.

NO GUILT HERE! TOO LITTLE, TOO LATE! AT 82, TIME IS OF THE ESSENCE IN MY MIND. WITH HIM, IT IS ALL ABOUT HIM.

I believe the diagnosis was manic/depressive with delusions. In other words, bat shit crazy.

I TRIED TO HELP HIM AS MUCH AS I WAS ABLE. WHAT A PHONY.

She is indignant about many things. She is also nuts.

Their pronouncements of how little they cared escalated until they just sounded the same. EVEN IF I WAS DYING I

WOULDN'T CROSS THE STREET TO SPEAK TO HIM, she wrote to me in an email. At Thanksgiving dinner, he began to say, *If she was choking on a dog bone on the other side of the street*—and all I could do was laugh. They both kept saying the other was *dead to me*, that phrase exactly, which I'd never known anyone to use in earnest. But *dead* was the right word. They were obsessed with each other's absence. It was really not so different from mourning.

Her emails proliferated when she was in a good spell, usually in spring, and dried up when her mood got low again in the fall. I often wouldn't notice until my dad asked me if I'd heard from her lately. She lived alone, and nobody checked on her. So then I'd email her, and she'd respond, and I'd come back to him and say *She's alive*, and he'd go back to wishing her dead.

———

When people talk about the middle of nowhere, they talk about Iowa. When people talk about meat and crops, they talk about Iowa. Then, every four years, during the caucuses, the state celebrates a brief, beaming moment on the national stage, when its flatness becomes its greatest asset. Because Iowa seems so empty, it can be filled with any meaning people choose to make of it.

For a few decades, Iowa was a swing state. Before the Farm Crisis, it was a red state, but in 1988 it flipped to blue and stayed there for a while. All this meant, in numbers, was that a small contingent of voters had shrugged and checked a different box—and a much larger contingent had shrugged and checked the same one they always did. To pundits, though, the

small shift seemed miraculous. I got the sense that they imagined a farmer in overalls, nodding to speeches, changing his
mind. In 2016, when the state flipped back, everyone wanted
to know why the farmer had changed his mind again, assuming that change could be traced along a coherent path of persuasion. What I saw was not coherence or persuasion. It was, if
anything, a marginally heightened ambivalence.

Notably persuadable was not how I'd ever known Iowans
to be, or at least, it wasn't how I'd known my family. Early on,
Peggy chose her son as the principal wrong of her life; her son
chose money. Each wrong remained fixed in place, and logic
twisted around it. In childhood, Dad's mother wielded money,
then in college, the baton was briefly handed to the rich kids
that surrounded him, but soon after he swore to redistribute
his wealth, it became clear that becoming rich was far easier.
Thus the wrong stretched again: the principal crime of rich
kids shifted from their wealth to their coastal liberal elitism, the
cushy ideals they could afford to espouse. As wealth became a
reality for him, the wrong stretched its arms to accommodate
the poor, the middle class, immigrants, teachers' unions. Each
tax day, in their names, the government stole half his income.
Though he could live like a king on the half that remained, he
thought only of the half that they took. He renamed his loss
the economy, which tied his coffers to everyone's fate. To hurt *the
economy* would also hurt *the people*, and thus, in a few flicks of
logic, the most likely benefactors of a given reform could be
twisted into its most vulnerable victims.

The rest of his conservatism would dissolve if you held it to
the light. I can tell he doesn't really care whether a person prays

in school or aborts their fetus or gets gay-married. The economy is a god he both reveres and fears, but outside of it, the enemies his party urges him to take are to him like ants, like mice, their threat to him symbolic, his war with them a diversion. He is at heart a cowboy conservative, yearning to be riled but offended by little. The last time he voted was 1992 and it was for Ross Perot, a bombastic populist billionaire who won rare bipartisan support because his campaign was unpinned from meaning. By partisan standards, or even by the standards of naked capitalist greed, Perot's platform was contradictory. To the working and the middle and the ruling classes, to cashiers and farmers and tycoons, he made the same promise of rage and money.

February 2017, my second year of graduate school. I was lying in bed beneath a weighted blanket, a pile of Goldfish crackers on my chest. Iowa winters felt colder than any I'd experienced before, more frigid and mean than Illinois, than New Hampshire. Science offered no explanation for this feeling—supposedly, Iowa was about as cold as anywhere—so I cobbled together my own. I suspected that the corn that sweated into the atmosphere and made the summer air unbearable became in winter a pile of fallow, wet dirt that froze the air. Then there were the cows and pigs with their broad dim backs sucking up all the sun. There weren't as many tall buildings in Iowa and the wind, with nothing to slow its course, slapped your face with full polar force, or so I reasoned. Iowa was full of wind; it powered half the state. The turbines looked spectral when viewed across a vast soybean field, but when a single blade passed by you on a flatbed truck, a white fiberglass wing longer and quieter than a blue whale, you realized wind's terrifying power. Even though this was by now my sixth Iowa winter, it always came as a shock. Even under the Wirecutter-recommended blanket, I felt cold, and so I lay there on my phone shopping for a better blanket. There would always be a better one.

I flipped between my shopping cart and my email inbox, where I was composing a lengthy rebuttal to the latest article my dad had sent. This was our routine. He sent me an article from a fifth-rate conservative news website whose name sounded like a spam email. I spent a half hour writing an impassioned argument trying to prove him wrong. Sometimes, I filled my messages with numbers and experts. Sometimes, I used every synonym for *bad* I could conjure: *craven, virulent, brutish*. Sometimes, I would try soft entreaties, and sometimes, when I felt desperate, I tried their opposite: I spit that he was demonic, a disgrace, that exchanges like these would make his death hurt less. No matter what I hurled at him, he responded in a few short, unperturbed sentences, flicking my fervor away like a gnat, so assured was he of his beliefs that to defend them was beneath him. When I issued my rebuttals, I needed desperately to change his mind, because the consequences of his wrongness felt immediate and catastrophic, as corrosive to my sense of self as they were to the world at large. But when he forwarded me his articles, it was with the beatific smile of a Christian handing you a leaflet. He would've liked very much for me to join him, but my refusal said nothing about his faith. He wanted to convert me, but he didn't need to convince me, and besides, we both knew who I'd turn to when I really needed help. Just like I'd pray to God while doubled over on the toilet, I'd still call my dad outside a body shop to ask if the mechanic was lying, and then let him pay for the costly repair. I'd still show up for every holiday. Silence was the cruelest thing I could've done to him, and it never occurred to me. In the middle of writing a response to his latest email, another one dinged onto the screen. *Have you heard from grandma?*

I hadn't. I'd emailed her a few days ago with the subject *Storm Lake?* My younger brother told me he'd have the summer free, and I asked her if he and I could clean out the house. Cleaning wasn't the right word for what I really wanted to do, but my interest in the Storm Lake house had grown over the past year. I didn't know what I'd find in there, but the possibility of finding anything at all was enough.

She hadn't responded to my request, so I turned to her Facebook to look for signs of life. Her latest shared post was an ad for bear-repellent products. I hit play on the video, in which a man argued that grizzly infestations were overrunning our schools. The repellent he sold was a jar of glitter. An obvious joke, she'd posted it earnestly—not because she believed what she saw, but because she never even watched it. I could tell that she never watched or read anything she shared, because sometimes, she posted articles that plainly refuted her conservative beliefs but whose headlines, at a glance, might appear to validate them. This post was like all the others. In each one she saw, twinned neatly together, a threat and its cure, and her reflex to neutralize the threat was so strong that she didn't stop to consider whether it had ever existed.

Ever since the election, we'd been talking less. It wasn't so much that I felt newly betrayed by her—she'd become a Tea

Partier years ago and never looked back. But until now, her views had felt more idiosyncratic, more fringe, more like conspiracy theories than political ideology, and so I dismissed them as extensions of her own troubled brain, which I understood far more intimately and sympathetically than the political movement to which she now belonged. In my dad's politics I saw a callous selfishness, but in hers, I saw pain. Come November, it became clear that I'd been wrong twice. First, their views were not fringe, nor idiosyncratic, and if they were a reflection of internal disorder, then that disorder was not unique to her, nor him, but shared by millions, and what was a shared disorder if not a bona fide ideology? Second, he was in pain too, but what good was this knowledge? I'd spent so long trying to understand my family, but I'd never stopped to consider what I'd do once I had it. Whether or not I understood why it was broken, the brain inside their brain was still their brain. What they thought was what they thought.

The bear post had been a week ago. There'd been no activity since then. I sent her an email with just a subject: *HELLO*. A few hours later, when she still hadn't responded, I followed up with *ARE YOU ALIVE?* Before I fell asleep, I tried again. *PLEASE RESPOND WE'RE WORRIED*. By the next afternoon, still nothing.

I emailed my dad:

She hasn't been online. What should we do?

He responded:

Perhaps she is dead.

We went back and forth like this. She had moved away from her Iowa friends to be closer to her family in Illinois, but we'd all left by now. I told my dad I didn't know Richard's number, or Linda's. I told him she wasn't picking up her phone. I asked him if he could send anyone to check on her, but my family wasn't the type to keep those kinds of people close by, the kind of people whom you trusted enough to ask for help. My parents bounced between their houses. They rarely spoke to neighbors, didn't put down roots. In order, they had each other, then their kids, then their dogs, and, further down, a handful of faraway friends and extended family members whom they called and emailed every so often. There was a mysterious spot in the center of their TV where everything turned greenish. Eventually, my brother figured out why: the screen was tuned to Fox News for so many hours a day that the relentless parade of spray-tanned talking heads had made the orange pixels burn out.

Dad was angrier at his mom than he'd ever been. A few months earlier, she'd informed him that not only had she disinherited him, but now she was considering skipping us too, putting her entire estate into a trust that only her future great-grandchildren could access. Even then, they could collect only the interest, never the principal, which would remain untouched in perpetuity. *The interest*, he seethed over Christmas dinner, *as if she's a Rockefeller*. She planned to die with a big number by her name, and now that number could long outlive her, her son, his children, their children. The theoretical pile of money had by now been gifted and rescinded and titrated so many times that these changes felt, to the rest of us, as arbitrary and immaterial as a terror alert. But the money was real to him. It was real to her. Nobody was dead to anybody. They were alive, aggrieved, and still smarting.

I kept asking what we should do until it became obvious that, as a family, *we* weren't going to do anything. The inertia, the little jokes, the ledger in which care and pain always stood even. The laws of our love had never been clearer. I imagined her lying in a pile of old magazines, taking ragged breaths. I sat on my bed shivering, and finally called the police. A female officer picked up. They had made contact with my grandma, yes. Someone else, the woman wouldn't say who, had called in a wellness check. I kept asking where she was, but the woman couldn't legally tell me. She sounded exasperated, but at some point, something made her reconsider. Quietly, underlining each word, she told me to try the hospital closest to my grandma's house.

I dialed the front desk, which connected me to another desk, then a nurse in psychiatrics who told me yes, she was here. Telephone hours had ended, but she would make an exception. And suddenly, for the first time in years, I was hearing my grandma's voice. She told me that her doctor's office had called the police after something she said on the phone—she didn't tell me what—alarmed them. The police had come, and she'd been taken to the hospital. I considered but didn't ask the word *voluntarily?* Talking to her, I felt the kind of relief that describes old sculptures. Carved out of the same material as my background, even as I stood outside it. Scooped out.

After a few days, she returned home, new prescription in hand. Her Facebook quickly roared back to life. I imagined her lying in bed in her condo, sharing and sharing and sharing.

Sometimes I wanted to cry for her. Sometimes I wanted to claw my DNA out of my arm with my bare hands. In her posts, the grandma of saccharine platitudes nestled side by side with the grandma of paranoid fury, and I saw in neither of them the grandma I knew. She wasn't a cookies grandma or a yelling grandma. She was a grandma of gentle oddities, humored curiosity. I saw her in the grainy photo of quartered soap bars that announced the surprising reason why a woman was putting Irish Spring in her yard. I saw her in the list of no-bake desserts. I didn't see her in the Mother's Day poem, nor in the foamy-mouthed headlines, but in the way it felt to scroll back and forth between them until they blurred together, fervent, fearful, brimming above all.

Your Mother is always with you.

IF YOU EAT TODAY, THANK A FARMER. IF YOU EAT IN PEACE, THANK A VETERAN.

She's the cool hand on your brow when you're not feeling well, she's your breath in the air on a cold winter's day.

MOM OF 3 EVADES HUMAN TRAFFICKERS IN IKEA

She is the sound of the rain that lulls you to sleep, the colors of a rainbow, she is a Christmas morning.

TEENAGE GIRL BURNED ALIVE BY BLACK GANG, NO MEDIA OUTRAGE

Your mother lives inside your laughter.

LOCALS FLEE AFTER MIGRANTS MASTURBATED INTO JACUZZI, DEFECATED INTO KIDS POOL.

She's the place you came from, your first home, the map you follow with every step you take.

FI YUO CNA RAED TIHS, YUO HVAE A SGTRANE MNID TOO.

She's your first love, your first friend, even your first enemy, but nothing on earth can separate you.

THE MOST DANGEROUS LIARS ARE THOSE WHO THINK THEY ARE TELLING THE TRUTH.

Not time, not space ... not even death.

Shrink

BEAUTY IS A GROWTH INDUSTRY, so said my CEO. She was new to the company, like me, having only arrived during the last fiscal quarter. Before that, she sold cell phones, and before that, McDonald's, and years ago, Cap'n Crunch and Rice-A-Roni. Now she sold makeup, or I sold it for her, or it sold itself.

Though my store carried several high-end brands, it lacked the luxury pedigree of Sephora, its biggest competitor. You could see it in the bags—theirs, a glossy black that stood up on its own, ours, a pale orange sack. Sephora was the wife of Moses, she who declared her husband the bridegroom of blood after circumcising her son with a flint knife, her name derived from Hebrew, *little bird*. Ulta is *ultra* without an *r*.

My store split its inventory into five basic categories: makeup, skincare, body, hair, and nails. From there, all products were reduced to one of two classes: mass or prestige. The former meant drugstore. The latter meant expensive. Prestige makeup, hair care, and skincare occupied the store's upper right quadrant, and mass, its left. Shelves of nail polish marked the boundary between prestige face and prestige hair. Hair tools, both mass and prestige, intermingled in the lower left. The salon abutted them. Fragrances rose along the back prestige wall. The registers were neither a supermarket-style row of parallel bays, nor a station along the wall. Instead, they sat around a ring-shaped counter in the middle of the store, arranged so as to be nearly panoptical. We stood anchoring the center.

I started at Ulta in October, having graduated from college the previous May. I'd spent the summer in Chicago getting rejected for unpaid positions at music agencies and copywriting jobs at Groupon, only to crawl back to my parents in August. While I was in college, they made a permanent move to the South Carolina beach town we had vacationed in for much of my childhood. To me, it was a place without time or adulthood or anything but heat and stillness. My mom picked me up from the airport. We passed the Towne Centre mall in landlocked Mount Pleasant, with its twelve-foot-tall stone horses standing sentinel in front of the P.F. Chang's. We ascended the sloping bridge that connected Mount Pleasant to the island beach town where my parents lived, at the top of which sat an American flag and, for a tall minute, a sweeping view of the Atlantic Ocean. We pulled onto the island's main drag, lined with palms and clogged with tourists, the pickups and surfboard-laden jeeps trundling along in a slow parade. We turned onto their street, which was a half mile long, no curbs or sidewalks, just a short strip of asphalt bookended by the ocean on one side and marshland on the other. Since the '90s, houses there were required to be built on stilts so that hurricanes could, rather than sweep the houses away, simply flow through them unobstructed. An old, thick pug stood still in the middle of the street, staring at our car as we veered around him. *That's just Dudley*, my mom said, driving past. My parents' right-hand neighbors had a dolphin-shaped fountain in their yard. Their left-hand neighbors owned a small bungalow that sat flat on the ground, which meant it had survived Hurricane Hugo. Between me and my parents' front door was a long flight of stairs and a fifty-pound suitcase. I lifted the suitcase gently over the first stair. I could feel beads of sweat forming already on my neck and rolling down my spine into my ass. The air felt like morning breath. Lugging the suitcase up the second stair, I let my arms slacken a little, then on the third stair a little more, until I was dragging the thing behind me, letting it bang violently on every single step. *You know I hate that*, my mom sighed. I reached the top, breathing hard as I shoved through the stacks of Amazon boxes that would be replaced by a new batch the next day. By the time I started punching in the door code, I'd lost all sense of forward motion. I was again a bored and restless child.

My sleep schedule quickly reversed itself. I would wake up as my parents ate dinner and go to sleep to the sounds of my dad making his morning SodaStream. I didn't need money but I did need a job, any job, something to differentiate living with my parents at age twenty-three from living with my parents at age fourteen. I applied to and proceeded to hear nothing back from Applebee's, Target, Costco, H&M, the Container Store, Panda Express, an ice cream cart at the zoo, and Urban Outfitters, which required that I take a personality assessment, the sole purpose of which seemed to be divining if and under what circumstances I would be stoned at work.

Only Ulta called me in for an interview. I sat down with Melanie, who had crimpy blond hair that she clipped half up, a southern accent, and the type of black, stretchy, flared trousers that are marked at $89.99 but always on sale for $59.99 under names like *The Aubrey* and *The Blythe* and are, somehow, the uniform of every female retail manager at every mall store across the country. She didn't ask me many questions, but when she looked at my résumé and saw that I'd majored in English, she asked what my future plans were. I paused. My parents had told me to conceal anything that might suggest I had an exit strategy. Ulta, they reminded me, did not want a liberal arts girl with rich parents for whom retail was merely a way to kill time on the way to Brooklyn, graduate school, or both. I'd learned this in high school when I'd looked for summer jobs only to find that summer jobs didn't really exist anymore, because the people who fill them don't really exist. If you have money, your summer job is pre-collegiate grooming rituals, all your unpaid internships and philanthropy. If you don't have money, your summer job is the job you already have. Ulta wanted someone who was likely to stay put. Ulta's ideal employee was someone who needed Ulta more than Ulta needed her. But in the moment, with my nose ring in my pocket, I panicked and accidentally told the truth. *I kind of want to be a writer.* She nodded politely.

Our store was located in the upscale-but-not-luxury Towne Centre outdoor shopping mall in the upscale-but-not-luxury town of Mount Pleasant, which was nearly on the water, but not quite. The town is nestled among old-money Charleston, with its million-dollar prewar mansions, some midsize middle-class towns, and a handful of small fishing villages. Mount Pleasant had itself been a small village, but 1931 brought the highway and 1989 brought the hurricane, which decimated the barrier islands. In Hugo's wake were insurance payouts and talk of new beginnings and, quickly, a real estate boom that never really ended. By the early 2000s its population doubled and became predominantly upper middle class. The new mall opened. Another highway was built. Now, ten years later, its population had doubled again and was sliding toward rich. Not quite Rich rich—Rich rich being an ineffable, ancient stratum of culture and wealth in which almost nobody in America believes themselves to reside—but statistically rich, the kind of rich that thinks it's upper middle class because it eats at the same chain restaurants as the masses.

On my first day at Ulta, I descended from my parents' gleaming SUV and walked among the rest of the gleaming SUVs looping endlessly through the Towne Centre's sprawling parking lot, their reflections shimmering across the windows of the Ann Taylor Loft, the Qdoba, the Hairy Winston Pet Boutique. The white pavement and the shiny cars seemed to magnify the sunlight. It was unseasonably warm that day, so hot the air looked wavy. The brief interludes of heat between icy car and icy store came as a series of shocks to the body, which may in fact be the entire point of outdoor malls: reminding you of your good fortune to be alive in the age of central air.

Dawn, the assistant manager, ushered me to the back room. I wore black pants and a black blouse I'd had to buy from the Old Navy next door. All of my other shirts either had non-sanctioned colors or had been cropped with scissors. My hair was a strange auburn color, the aftermath of a DIY bleach job I'd done a few months ago after watching *Spring Breakers*. I'd put my nose ring back in after the interview, and Dawn eyed it. *That's fine*, she said, aiming to reassure herself as much as me, *you're allowed one facial piercing*.

I sat on a folding metal chair as Dawn hit play on a training video. She handed me a headset. The Ulta CEO welcomed me to the family. A robotic female voice told me how to enter my time.

She stood next to me as my first customer approached. In life, my voice is boyish and jocular, but the one that came out was a breezy trill. *Did you find everything today?* I cooed. Nobody had taught me this phrase or this voice. *It's her first day*, Dawn explained as I tried to remember what to press on the register screen. *Thanks for bearing with us*, I said. Nobody had taught me to say *us*.

I relished the novelty. I'd always been a shopper, never a seller, and I delighted each time the curtain was pulled back. I learned about the locked perfume cage in the back. I learned new names for the mundane: theft was *shrink*, a thief was a *Thelma*, free products were *gratis*, a customer was a *guest* and an item they plucked from the shelf and later abandoned was a *go back*, checkout was the *cash wrap*, a shelf was positioned by a *planogram*, a shelf was positioned *by mandate from on high*, a shelf was a *gondola*, a shelf was an *endcap*, a shelf was an *étagère*. I learned the satisfaction of a workday that dissolved in an instant. The sweet finality of clocking out. I learned just how pale my skin and just how pink my cheeks were. I learned the acute chemical effect of being called pretty a few times a week.

It is perhaps a mark of my comfortable upbringing that the prospect of working retail excited me. But it is also something else. For Christmas one year, my older brother received a toy cash register. I think the idea was to make math fun for him. He abandoned the register after a few hours, but I didn't. I rang things up well into the evening—I sold myself a Lego, a pop-up book, a wheel for my doomed hamster, a petrified piece of licorice. The items were beside the point. It wasn't the things that I loved so much as the transaction, the beep of the buttons, the receipt paper smooth between my thumb and forefinger. The way the machine shivered when the cash drawer clicked shut. A friend of mine once declared smoking the perfect sensory experience: you smell it, touch it, fingers, lungs, hot on the inhale, visible on the exhale. It is perfect because your nerves sharpen, then calm. You witness the fact of your steady breathing. You make a habit of it.

Guests who belonged to our loyalty program earned ULTAmate Rewards Points with every dollar they spent. Compared to Sephora, whose Beauty Insider program exchanged dollars not for discounts but for deluxe samples, Ulta's rewards system was thought to be better, as it provided the illusion of savings. At the time, spending $250 at Sephora got you three-twentieths of an ounce of Intenso Pour Homme. The same sum at Ulta saved you, on the dollar, three-hundredths of a cent.

You needed one hundred points before you could get a discount. *I'm sorry*, I learned to say to those with fewer, *you haven't yet reached the threshold for redemption.* A guest's point balance was always displayed to me at checkout, but on my first day I was warned never to divulge this freely, at least not before they swiped. *The points are an incentive for guests to spend more*, said Melanie. *If you give that up before they pay, it's just a free discount.*

Instead, I was to do this: Print the receipt and smooth it flat on the counter. Lean over. Underline the fine print. *Here is a link to our guest satisfaction survey. You could win a $500 gift card.* Raise my eyebrows as if suddenly impressed. *Wow.* Circle a number at the bottom. *Looks like you have 732 points. That's almost $30 off.* Guest frowns. Wait. Couldn't I have used that today? *Well.* Conspiratorial. *Just another excuse to come back soon.* With my neon highlighter I drew a wonky heart.

The slickness of my little script felt balletic. It was a good kind of alien. Soon, stock phrases became mantras, became prayers, became muscle memory. *Hi there, If you could just swipe one more time, I apologize for the wait, Are you a rewards member, I'll take the next guest, You have a great day!* I could do it in my sleep.

———

In a pre-holiday staff meeting, assistant manager Dawn taught us the art of the pitch. We were each given an index card with a product's name. We were divided into pairs and told to role-play as guest and sales associate. The associate would ask leading questions to divine what was on the guest's index card, which was meant to represent their singular unrealized desire. It was our job to show the guests what they already wanted. Rachel's index card said *Hempz*, an organic body cream. The litany began. *Are we shopping for anyone in particular?* My niece. *Does she like hair?* No. *Does she like makeup?* Her skin is dry. *Some lotion then?* Yeah. *Does she like sweet scents?* No. *Musky?* No. *What does she like?* Dawn called for everyone to wrap up. *What does she like?* Rachel frowned, flustered, before offering: *Weed?*

Dawn addressed the room. *Some people get shy about it. They tell me, "It feels like I'm selling them something." And I say, well,* she snorted, *you are.*

I am not shy. For as long as I've had a voice, I have loved the sound of it. At five I talked to the dog. At six to a tape recorder. At seven to the mirror, pretending to be in a Neutrogena commercial. I filled my cupped hands with water, threw the water in my face, over and over murmuring *cream cleanser, cream cleanser, cream cleanser.* I held up a single Mike and Ike in the back corner of a pizza restaurant and pretended to sell Tylenol to the wall. Later, I began to mimic the beauty YouTubers I watched. They all knew to speak in the same strange cadence. *The* was pronounced *thee*, the article *a* became *ay.* They spoke the same way I did when I interviewed myself on my Little Tikes tape recorder. It was a clicky, rhythmic pleasure, like a girl who has just gotten fresh acrylics and uses them to punctuate her speech. There is no way to represent it without musical notation.

So I <u>went</u> online andpick<u>tup</u> thee <u>Tarte</u> Amazonian Clayyyy . . . Blush? In thee shade Seduce? It izzay pinky. Mauvey. <u>Nude :)</u>

At my store we sold products with names like *Bye Bye Pores* and *Better Than Sex*, which is a twenty-three-dollar tube of water and wax. We sold face powders in *Warmth* and *Poured Moonstone*, and not one but three One Direction perfumes named, respectively, *Our Moment, That Moment,* and

You & I. Whenever confused husbands came in looking for "some Naked palette," I explained to them that there were actually seven Urban Decay *Naked* eyeshadow palettes, and I could, when called upon, spend a good thirty minutes discussing the relative merits of each. A shelf of headbands gathered dust in the neglected center aisle. A sodden cotton ball was stuffed between liquid luminizers. A pink-ribboned curling iron announced its benevolence. For a fee, one of our trained professionals could extend your eyelashes. For a limited time, Mandy could rhinestone your brows. You could buy lipstick in shades *Shame* and *Dominatrix* and a few feet away, genuine human growth hormone at $99 a box. A droop-eyed woman with lipstick bleed told me at checkout that it made her hair fall out. I nodded and gave her store credit.

Ulta sold a liquid lipstick called Beso, a true neutral red, and I became the reason it was out of stock. When I wore it, I sold, on average, three tubes of the stuff, just by smiling at the register. It was an acute, specific power. One woman was on the phone with her bank as I rang her up. As she was about to swipe, she put her hand over the speaker, stage-whispered *What lipstick is that,* and bought it on the spot. I mostly worked the cash wrap, not the sales floor, but lipstick remained my best shill. Whenever I could, I'd swatch the shades side by side on my hand, knowing full well my body sold the pitch. Sometimes, a hand was too small, and I'd clock out with stripes running clear to my elbow. I loved it when my voice sold. The sweet lull of hearing yourself talk crystallizes into an almost narcotic rush when your reverie draws cash. Whenever I'd convince a guest to spend ten dollars on an ugly little breast cancer trinket, or apply for an ill-advised Ulta credit card, I floated to the ceiling. My audience hadn't just listened. They'd bought.

I sold things I didn't own. I sold things I didn't like. I sold things to people who were already buying them. It felt right, somehow, to compliment the customer's impulses. To confirm them. It felt like the store's final act of magic, to transform want into need. *This is really a must-have*, I'd say as I scanned the bar-code. *We can't seem to keep it in stock.* For a two-week period, a certain brand of rosemary-scented anti-lice children's shampoo flew off the shelves. *It's always the clean ones*, I'd say to the weary moms, beaming reassuringly as if shaking hands at a leper colony. I sometimes sold people to themselves, an act we also call a compliment when it's done for free. I rang up a tall, skinny, slightly awkward-looking teenager and asked her, wide-eyed, if she was a model. Ulta employees do not work on commission. I worked on something else.

Thanksgiving was rapidly approaching. Sometimes I worked with Teri, who was a full-time CPA but worked at Ulta most Saturdays. Teri was short, blue-black-haired, in her mid-fifties, and interminably jolly. Teri warned me that all the weirdos came out during the holidays. *They're not our regular customers—they don't act the same.*

At 3 a.m., Thanksgiving turkey still warm in my gut, I began my Black Friday shift. I expected madness, fistfights in the aisles, but it was really just more people. For two weeks, my shifts had been a blur of the shrieking fire alarm, which kept going off without cause, and the song "Chandelier" by Sia. On Black Friday, the alarm went off again, this time for thirty minutes. A woman asked Melanie what was going on. *Maybe it's all these red-hot savings*, I interjected. The woman laughed, Melanie did not. They were both my boss.

Then the power went out. *Is Bed Bath & Beyond out?* Dawn implored. The Bed Bath & Beyond next door was a major player in the Towne Centre mall. If they fell, we all did. My coworker Lindsay and I looked at her blankly. We hadn't been outside in ten hours. A guest who'd just left the Beyond told us their power had come back. Then ours came back. I heard the opening bars of "I Love It" by Icona Pop, which sounded like the fire alarm. The actual fire alarm continued to blare. A woman came to the cash wrap looking frazzled. I asked her for her phone number, as I did all members of our rewards program. *I don't have one*, she said. *Our house just burned down.* At the end of my eleven-hour shift, Dawn's voice came over the headset—*Why did someone wheel a shopping cart in here? We need to get that out of here.*

Never mind, she said with resignation a few minutes later, *they've got a baby in it.*

———

When Teri said our holiday customers were not like our regular customers, I wasn't sure what she meant. Many of our regular customers were rich—not yacht rich, or summer-as-a-verb rich, but rich enough that Dawn called guest relations *putting on your Mount Pleasant.*

Our rich customers adopted a mask of good-natured surprise when I told them their totals, sometimes stage-whispering down to their children, *We won't tell Daddy about this.* Our rich customers rarely paid cash, but when they did, they used $100 bills. *I've never seen so many of these in my life*, I said to Dawn. *Yeah, well*, she replied, *welcome to Mount P*. A few weeks after I started at Ulta, a video of a woman's customer-service rant went viral. Angela's search for an out-of-stock Bath & Body Works candle had culminated in a tense standoff with the store's manager, Jen. Jen had apologized, but Angela wanted more—a better apology, a free gift, a word with corporate, something to mark the spot where she had sought deference and been denied.

Years later, the world would become obsessed with people like Angela and give them a name: Karen, a breed of high-strung, entitled, affluent white woman who demanded servility from everyone around her. When everyone was talking about Karen, I thought back to Ulta. In telling us to put on our Mount Pleasant, my managers suggested that the degree of chipper, coddling deference we showed to the customers was directly proportional to their wealth. The richer you were, the more you wanted from us, the thinking went. But what I quickly noticed was that I acted the same no matter who the customer was. As long as they were buying something, they were also buying me. To be a service worker is to be in constant deference to Karens, yes. But in retail, a Karen can be anyone. Karen is a mindset born less of class, gender, or skin color than of the relationship between employee and customer, which is not unlike the relationship between product and customer. The rich were no more or less demanding of my hospitality, no more or less insistent that I go check in the back, no more or less indignant when the crumpled $3.50 coupon they'd fished out of their purse did not apply to their purchase because, as I had to explain several times a day, those coupons never applied to prestige products, only mass.

We want to believe that Karen's sense of entitlement is unique to her privilege, that only a profound alienation from the suffering of other people would allow her to act so inhumane. *Clearly*, people would comment beneath Angela's video, *this lady has never worked a service job*. But it seemed just as likely to me that Angela and Jen shared a socioeconomic class, that Angela *had* worked a job like this, maybe even that she *did* work one now. I saw it all the time on Yelp, where reviewers foregrounded their disgust by noting that they worked in the very same industry. It seemed to me that one store's angry customer could easily become another store's patient manager, and vice versa, that Jen could become Angela and Angela could become Jen, that they could seesaw forever, on the clock and at the bottom, off the clock and looking down.

———

Liberal arts college had been like a summer program for gifted and talented youth, in that my parents paid large sums of money to have my specialness tested and validated through a series of guided activities. I was asked again and again to prove my worth, the assumption being that I had it in vast quantities. Working retail is the exact opposite. You are presumed unspecial the moment you don a name tag, a smock, a novelty visor. You are the public face of the company, a sentient billboard–cum–cash register, and your studied unspecialness—your ability to cede, to blend, to empty—is, in fact, your greatest strength. I knew this before I ever worked a service job, but it still came as a shock. Once, I accidentally shorted a guest $20 in change on her $100 bill and realized it only after she'd left. I agonized over my mistake for an hour, imagining her squinting at her receipt, then back to her wallet, then back to the receipt, cursing my name. When she returned an hour later, I kept repeating *I am so sorry, I am so dumb, I am so sorry, I am so dumb.* When she smiled and said *Everybody makes mistakes*, it was as if I was learning the aphorism for the first time. I had been granted grace. I wanted to kiss her feet.

Ulta was the first time I'd been paid to do anything, and I'd never felt less valuable.

The novelty of being a product had begun to twist. Two weeks before Christmas, an older woman approached me looking for lip gloss in a natural pink—the industry calls this an MLBB: My Lips But Better. I launched into a list of several different formulas, all of which I *absolutely loved*. I finished my spiel and she asked, smiling, what shade of MLBB *I* was wearing. My chirp dissolved in my throat, my real voice flowing back low and quiet as I told her *Oh, these are just my lips. Well,* she rolled her eyes, *isn't that nice for you.*

One day, a guest complimented my eyes, so I jumped the gun and secretly redeemed her one thousand points for a fifty-dollar discount. Highlighter in hand, I showed her what I'd done, warm with the generosity of my small corporate rebellion. But she was angry. She had been saving her points. She wanted them back. To restore the balance, she would have to return each item and then purchase it anew. Silently, solemnly, she watched me perform our transaction in reverse.

During my first week, I forgot Melanie's name, and when I asked her, with an apologetic smile, to remind me, she narrowed her winged eyes. *You forget your boss's name?* The second time, I accidentally called her Dawn. From then on, my fate was sealed. I couldn't tell if she just thought I was dumb or if she could smell it on me, the luxury of not having to care whether my boss liked me, the fact that I belonged to the demographic of my customers and not my coworkers, that I didn't need to be good at the job, for it was as consequential to my livelihood as a weekend pottery class. But the thing was, I still cared. I didn't need to be a good worker, but I still wanted to be one, desperately.

Dawn—saltier, funnier, lowlier in managerial status—I got along with better, until one day in the break room. Lindsay and I were chitchatting, and I mentioned how I'd learned that, in the state of California, employees got paid lunch. *I wish we got paid lunch,* I said wistfully as I poked at my Southwest chicken salad. Suddenly, like a poltergeist, Dawn appeared at my side. *Say goodbye to the dollar menu,* she sputtered. Lindsay and I looked at her quizzically. *You wanna pay more for a hamburger?* she intoned. Lindsay and I said nothing still. *If people don't want to work at McDonald's,* she continued, *then go to college and become the CEO of McDonald's.*

She probably thought you were trying to unionize, my dad explained over dinner. Dawn probably made a pittance too, but her pittance was still our pittance doubled, and she fought for it more viciously than the smirking CEOs who appeared as talking heads on my dad's Fox News shows. Those men seemed to shoo labor rights away calmly, almost genially, so assured were they of their winning hand. From then on, Dawn was a Melanie too.

As Christmas loomed closer, I began spending almost all my time on register, not floor, and my charisma with custom-

ers was becoming a liability; my guest relations were too slow.
I was there to grease the wheels of each transaction, nothing more. I needed to trim the chatter until I was checking guests out in two minutes or less. At the time, we were raising money for breast cancer research. A ten-dollar donation got you a clutch or a bracelet. Melanie said we could root around the gratis box if we sold ten of them in a shift, an incentive that seemed less for charity than for the considerably larger gratis I suspected Melanie would get if her store won. Melanie told us to adjust the language we used—instead of *Do you want to donate to breast cancer research* we should try *Would you care to donate* or *Can I count on you to donate.* I didn't know what was in the gratis box, but I knew I wanted it.

One day, a guest told me that she already donated a portion of her paycheck to breast cancer research. *I'm a survivor,* she said. *So is my mom,* I responded, which was true, so I said it in my real voice. We talked for another minute or two. The moment the guest turned to leave, Dawn marched out from the back room with her jaw clenched. Though there were fifty minutes left in my shift, she told me to go home.

My shifts became more sporadic. Sixteen hours one week, thirty-two the next. The exhaustion I felt when I clocked out surprised me. At an office job, you have to dress a certain way, arrange your face into certain shapes, pitch your voice clearer and higher, clench your butt cheeks tighter when you walk through the hallways to your warm little desk chair. Jobs like Ulta demand the same, except there is nowhere to lean. There is no cubicle, no backstage where you can let your entire body slump, and most important, no comfortable salary on which to

hang your exhaustion. There are just things to sell, people to
buy them, and you. The customer is king, the CEO is divine,
and between them, like an isthmus, stretches your cheerful
smile. I bought gel insoles. I began to apply antiperspirant to
my neck. I learned that guests actually took our guest satisfaction survey. *I drove VERY FAST from my job,* one wrote, *and
your shelves looked like WALMART.* We'd gotten low marks on
door greeting, but the store was kept purposefully understaffed,
so Melanie just added it to the cashiers' duties. My voice went
hoarse from screaming *Welcome in!* over the din. I began to hate
how much I hated the job, how I felt ground down by each
small indignity, how I felt lowly for not having a sales floor
position, how I'd catch myself scrubbing the toilets with too-
small rubber gloves and thinking *I don't deserve this,* as if there
were people who did. I learned that my heart raced with too
many eyes on me. I learned a customer's request that we *check
in the back* would almost never yield the requested product, that
when we *checked in the back* we were really just staring for five
minutes at our phones or a wall because the back did not contain rows of stocked shelves so long they merged into the horizon like industrial chicken cages, but rather a cement rec room
with harsh lighting containing the remnants of several takeout lunches, unused promotional displays, and a bulletin board
onto which management had tacked a grainy black-and-white
surveillance shot of two women exiting the store, ostensibly
to warn us about these professional thieves lest they return,
but really to remind us that we were the store's most probable
thieves. If anyone could beat us at our many-fingered game, it
was them, the thieves who paid us.

It was not Dawn or Melanie who fired me, but the bulletin board. When they posted the new schedule, I noticed that I had only a shift on Thursday of that week, and then not at all the next week. When I asked Melanie about it, she tilted her head, not unkindly. *Emily, you're observant in a way that's good for a writer. Not for a sales associate.* I asked her, hesitantly, if that meant I was fired. *Well, it's January*, she responded, *and you're seasonal.* The season was over.

When I refer to Ulta now, I get the urge to call it *my alma mater*, an urge I don't have with the actual college from which I graduated. Maybe it's because there is no lofty way to say *my old job*. I avoided entering that Ulta for years, but when I finally returned, nobody I knew was working there. The store looked completely different too—Ulta had capped off a banner fiscal quarter by revamping dozens of locations. Mass and prestige weren't separated anymore, and the cash wrap now sat along the wall. Later, I looked Melanie up on Facebook. She was pregnant. She was doing something with real estate. She'd posted a selfie. Her lips were a bright, matte red, a true red, not too blue and not too orange. A friend of hers had commented: *What lipstick is that?* Melanie had replied: *Beso by Stila.*

Bailey, a third-tier manager who joined in November and whose role remained unclear, was the only other person working on my last day at Ulta. We closed together. She asked me to clean the bathrooms, which I'd like to call symbolic, but it was only procedure. I had already decided what I was going to steal. I knew where the cameras were, where they weren't, which items had anti-theft stickers, and most important, I knew that the camera footage, due to understaffing, was rarely, if ever, reviewed. I slipped the items into the go-backs basket, stuffed the go-backs basket into a dark corner, and tucked the items in my bra. In the bathroom, I unwrapped them: a face brush that promised *optical blurring*, and a bright red lip pencil in a shade called *Bang*. The safest way to steal was to hide the object in dark, tender places where no decent person would root. I walked out of the bathroom with the brush and the pencil nestled tightly against my crotch. All that was left between me and the outside world were the tall, gray anti-theft pillars. I stepped toward them, wincing, bracing myself for the beep.

For guests, the beep meant nothing. Though the threat of theft defined many of our rituals, the guests were insulated from suspicion. We were forbidden from chasing customers out of the store. We were functionally forbidden from confronting them in-store too, allowed to do so only if we could keep the customer in an unbroken line of sight. *If they turn a corner or go behind a shelf*, Dawn warned, *you can't say anything. They could've put the thing back.* If the pillars beeped for a customer, they would look back at the cash wrap either nervous or irritated, and we'd wave them through regardless.

The gray pillars had beeped for me once as an employee. When it happened, I panicked, though I had stolen nothing. I dug into my pockets, patted myself down like the TSA, pulled out every item in my clear plastic tote bag, the same kind required in stadiums to ensure you don't sneak in outside food or a handgun. *My sweater*, I'd panted finally to Melanie, who didn't seem fazed either way, *they forgot to take the tag off my sweater.*

━━━

Six years later, I stood in line at a Las Vegas Target. In my cart were eighty dollars of overpriced groceries and a nail polish

I'd decided, at the last minute, not to steal. I noticed a group of teenage boys approaching the checkout with armfuls of Grey Goose and Patrón bottles. When they got up to the registers, they walked right past, their steps purposeful but unhurried. They continued heading toward the door. Everyone—the customers, the cashiers, the security guards—stood still and watched in awe. As the teenagers stepped through the pillars, the alarm sounded. Nobody bolted, nobody hid. They knew the beep meant nothing. The store couldn't chase them if it wanted to. Crossing the threshold, one of them turned back around to face the crowd, gripping the necks of the bottles and raising them into the air as he bellowed *WE DON'T GIVE A FUCK*. The alarm kept beeping as the boys walked out into the sunshine. I'd never heard a feebler sound.

If the gray pillars beeped as I left work on that final day, I planned to bolt through them and head for the parking lot, to run until I was a customer again. But they didn't make a sound. As I began to push the doors open, almost in the clear, Bailey held out her arm to stop me. I froze. *Bag check*, she said dully. I'd forgotten. I opened my tote and she peered down into it. She nudged aside two tampons, a fork from home, a water bottle from the break room vending machine. She stopped when she found a tube of Lipstick Queen lipstick that I'd bought from Ulta years earlier, before I ever worked there. Then she turned it upside down, searching for the dot. On my first day, Melanie had marked the bottom of the tube with a green dot of paint so that every time she checked my bag, she'd know I hadn't stolen it. Dots were also given to my glass pot of concealer and my bottle of rosewater face spray. When I bought a tube of hand cream with my employee discount, it got a dot too. If I owned anything that Ulta sold, the dot was the only thing that let it cross between the two worlds, the one where Ulta belonged to me and the one where I belonged to Ulta. I still have the lipstick, and it still has the dot, which was made to show that it was mine, it was mine and not theirs, not theirs but on loan to them, until I clocked out.

Testimonial

Years ago, while browsing for faux-kilim throw pillows online, I clicked, out of habit, on a product I already owned. I glanced between the pillow on my bed and its twin on my screen, the consumer version of looking at yourself in the mirror to make sure you're still alive. And then, I read the reviews. *Great Pioows*, said one person. *Set means you get one, seriously???????* said another. As I continued to scroll, another review caught my eye. The title: *Cute but scratchy*.

> Loved the way the pillow looked, and I was impressed with its heft; it definitely isn't flimsy. However, the fabric on the front is really scratchy, so if you want people to put their faces or bare skin on this, I would think twice.

I nodded along with the reviewer, my tongue pressing excitedly against my teeth, one of those small, tense ways our bodies let off energy as we sit still before a glowing screen.

Yes! I thought. *The pillow is scratchy.* Why wasn't anyone else talking about this? It gave no comfort and felt like a rash. But in my agreement, I still smirked at the reviewer's tone. What kind of lady took throw pillows seriously enough to issue a warning about them? Even though she and I had both bought the pillow, had both cared enough to revisit it online like an old friend, she seemed, somehow, to care too much. She'd even used a semicolon. It was like I'd caught her masturbating or practicing her laugh in a mirror, a moment of private indulgence made unsettlingly public.

I finished reading and looked up to see the reviewer's name. A light dissociative mist clouded my vision as I noticed the name *Em* above the words I'd just read, and remembered, suddenly, that I was the one who had written them. Em, I realized with a jolt, was me. All along, I was the masturbator, I was the pillow vigilante, I was the lady who cared too much.

This had never happened to me before. If you pulled any sentence from my journals, I could recognize it instantly as mine, not because the style or content of my words is inimitable, but because I remember the physical effort of their making, in the same way you smell your own shit differently because you felt it come out of your body. My review had been written with care, perhaps more care than I'd ever applied to a journal entry; I cared very much about what it said. So why didn't I recognize it? The difference, I realized, was one of dominion. My personal writing came from me willingly, my mouth, my words. But my review, like a gospel, came through me unbidden. The voice was someone else's.

Before I quit writing online reviews for good, Em was the name I used for them. To use my full name was too close, and to make up a fake one seemed too great an admission of shame, so I used Em, a sheepish pseudonym. To post these grievances but mask them with Em was to participate in the same cycle of scrutiny and renunciation I engaged in when I was annoyed by, say, a girl at a café. With nowhere else to vent my frustration, wanting to be placated by other people's anger, I'd google *Listen without headphones public rude why Reddit*, and then immediately clear the search from my browser history. This wasn't a security measure; I knew nobody would ever go looking for this version of me, pinched and mundane. I was hiding her not from others but from myself. Em wasn't wrong about the world, but her beadiness still embarrassed me. I wanted her to notice less.

I was born Emily, and Emily was born with a list of what she trusted. The list was as long as the world. Slowly, she began to cross things off. She learned not to trust the continuity of floors, the stability of wobbly objects. Some trusts were traded for others, the trust that her mom would never leave replaced by the trust that she'd always come back. Then she learned about lies. Strangers who said they had candy or a puppy were lying, even if they really had the candy or the puppy—some lies were so big that they could still contain truths. A lie that called itself a lie wasn't a lie, like cartoons. But the ads between cartoons were like the candy and the puppy. These commercials might claim true things, but they always wanted something from you, and this want squirmed under the truths like worms beneath a rock.

All this seemed simple enough. But then the borders between ads and everything else began to dissolve, and it was hard to tell who wanted what. If Mischa Barton said a face wash was good in an ad, then I knew not to listen, but if she said the same thing in an interview, the words she spoke freely could still be an ad, it turned out. A celebrity dropped her purse outside a nightclub and a bottle of diet pills spilled out, but that wasn't an accident. That was an ad too. For a while, I trusted product reviews in magazines, because magazines had so many ads already that what came between them had to be real. But no, it was candy and puppies all the way through. Ads were algae that grew wherever money did: so powerful was the consumer dollar that any piece of media, at any time, could be courting it. Thus, even when these media weren't explicitly selling a product, the perceived neutrality of their opinions was unctuous at best. If you wanted to know the truth about a product, the only unbiased, unpaid sources were your friends and family. Everything else had worms underneath.

———

It's weird to call 1999 the turn of the century, but the language of new dawns is applicable to Epinions.com, which debuted in September of that year. That month, Fannie Mae announced it would ease credit requirements on mortgage loans to give more borrowers a shot at equity. The internet was young, Google just a year old, and democracy was in the air. The founders of Epinions envisioned their platform as a *Zagat-for-everything*, a site where consumers could read and write reviews on any product imaginable, from movies to shampoo to the Bible, and those reviews would be, for the first time, trustworthy. At the time, sites like Amazon and CNET were also dipping their toes in the review game by featuring so-called editorial reviews, but those were written by employees with a vested interest in making a sale. Consumer-submitted reviews barely existed on the early internet. Epinions was the first site dedicated solely to reviews by regular people. It was the consumer's public square.

I come from a family of noticers, and I watched my fourteen-year-old brother rise through the Epinions ranks on the heels of this shared legacy. He reviewed bikes and electronics, mostly. Other users would rate his reviews as *Trusted* or *Not Trusted*, and the more trust he earned, the more points he'd rack up, which eventually gained him both a reputation and a monthly check for a few dollars. This was the other revolutionary thing about Epinions: it paid. Not much, but something. Reviews earned one cent per click, but unlike with magazine reviews, the money didn't taint their credibility. If anything, it bolstered the sense that consumers' opinions were driven by neither profit nor personal catharsis. Instead, their reviews were a dispassionate and neutral service, like a public utility.

Meanwhile, in 2004, a tween as obsessed with cosmetics as with information, I began to rely on a review site called MakeupAlley that had been founded the same year as Epinions. The Alley girls were not like the magazine editors, whose glee infected everything. The Alley girls were nerdy and exacting, and they didn't fall for hype. They knew Maybelline Great Lash mascara was terrible even if it was the best-selling mascara in the country, and that Monistat anti-chafe cream was better than any expensive face primer. Often, I'd leave the website having decided *not* to buy something, its hype punctured by the smartest girls I knew. It felt like finally breaking through a fog. It felt like a hand had reached down and taken mine. Em was birthed in the Alley.

That same year, a man in San Francisco needed a new doctor and realized he didn't know where to find a good one. Yelp was born. Consumers had been reviewing products for a few years now, but Yelp's offering was novel. Now, they could also review restaurants, doctors, museums, things that offered not objects but services, things that you bought but couldn't hold in your hand. That's when my dad began writing reviews. For a long time, he spent money on objects only. In law school, there were no vacations or meals out, just his station wagon filled with As Seen on TV products and a mountain of credit card debt. A decade later, he had many more As Seen on TV products and no more credit card debt, but when my mom asked him if he wanted to go out to eat, his answer was the same: *Why?* If the basement flooded or the car transmission broke, he'd sit down with a manual and fight tooth and nail to hack it, because nothing chafed him more than paying someone to do something that he could do himself. He balked at the idea of paying a premium for experience, or convenience, for something as transient and intangible as time well spent.

When Yelp gave him a way to turn experiences into stuff, restaurants became his favorite pastime. He posted his reviews under the moniker IowaAttorney4647. His reviews were well reviewed. They were thorough and fair. He always knew when a new spot was opening, was eager to dissect the crispness of its side potatoes, the layout of its menu, the visual interest of its light fixtures. In the middle of a lackluster meal, my mom might comment on how the tables felt too crowded together, or the

AC was cranked too high, or she'd note, during a good one, how expertly the steak had been seared, how warm and attentive the server had been, and she would turn to my dad and tell him he should put that in the review. They crafted their critique as they chewed.

My dad was among a small and dedicated cadre of reviewers upon whom Yelp relied in its early days, a group who, like the Alley girls, were not paid for their reviews. When Amazon, Target, and a handful of other retailers began to solicit their own user reviews, unpaid, a strange thing happened: people wrote them anyway. Epinions had been built on the assumption that few would spend their wild and precious lives penning a treatise on their third-favorite dish soap simply for pleasure. But it turned out that most reviewers were not, in fact, in it for the money.

These sites compensated users in a different way. Reviews gave shape to the act of noticing, in the same way memory gives shape to the unconnected sensations that we call being alive. They transformed consumers into a community, their small observations into valuable discourse. Reviewers were armchair philosophers who had finally found their forum, hobbyists whose knowledge had now crowned them experts. They'd finally been rewarded for their attention, and so they traversed aisles and streets searching for new experiences to recount for their followers, new holy grails and vicious swindles, their reviews not mere feedback but catechism. In the Bible, they're called *a great cloud of witnesses*. Reviewers had already seen the Kingdom, and their experience reassuringly marked your own future path.

Two decades later, and the world is full of Ems. It's difficult not to be one: decades of military-grade advertising and an almost unfathomable breadth of choice have honed the modern consumer's reflexes. There are so many things to buy and so many people begging you to buy them, so many glossy start-ups and dentists who advertise like glossy start-ups, and so hungry and insidious is the onslaught that now, to be Em—to know why and how and if you like the things you choose to purchase—is more than an afterthought. It's the only way to know that you have any modicum of personal choice at all.

Em was not like Emily. Em peppered her reviews with phrases like *exceeds expectations* and *unparalleled* and *fairly good* and *actively unpleasant*. Em talked a lot about "par," and a subject's position relative to it. Emily might feel a little dumb reviewing a McDonald's beneath an underpass in South Carolina, but Em would do it, because the broken ice cream machine was a bald lie, and Em was a truth seeker. Em held other reviewers to a high standard of intellectual conduct, giving particularly good reviews a thumbs-up or rating them *helpful* or *funny* or *cool*. She held herself to that same standard. Her reviews were reasonable, exacting yet impersonal. She always stuck to the task at hand, always maintained the clarity to see the sum and the parts at once. She would never reprimand a server for tepid enthusiasm, never deduct a star for an item that shipped a little slow, because her job wasn't to penalize mistakes or litigate bad luck. She was aware of the distinction between malice and apathy. Em's job was to empty herself of both and to simply pay attention. All she asked of the things she consumed was that they pay her this attention back.

By the time I encountered Em's pillow review, I relied upon reviews to buy virtually anything. I pored over them in depth, each product page filled with thousands of words written by thousands of people, like a bright room bursting with voices. I learned what was wrinkle- or leak-prone, what was hard to assemble, what held up in the wash. I pinched and spread my fingers to regard the warp and weft of a woven charcoal dishcloth, the melted cheese on the new breakfast Quesarito, the poorly constructed left armpit of a rayon blouse as it tugged across a stranger's chest. I'd never been able to retain the start date of the Civil War, but I knew all the ways a sofa could be assembled and stuffed, the finer points of wood joinery, the gradations of high-resiliency polyurethane foam, the difference between sinuous and hand-tied springs. That I could not, on a graduate-student salary, afford to heed such distinctions, that my sofa cost $200 and its cushions crunched like shopping bags when you sat on them, this was immaterial. I needed to become an expert in any desire I had, even ones I couldn't yet fulfill, so that when the time came, I'd be armed with knowledge. If I navigated to a product page and scrolled down to find that no reviews existed, it was as if the bright, crowded room had emptied and gone dark. I was back in the cave with the rocks and the worms. Anything could be a lie in there. I'd click away immediately.

———

To spend money on something means that you're beholden to it, but also that the thing is beholden to you. It owes you pleasure. Or comfort. Or adventure. It owes you a fulfillment

of need. More than a century ago, long before reviews revo-
lutionized the manner in which customers could be satisfied,
the concept of customer satisfaction was, itself, revolutionary.
Before the explosion of industry, if you didn't produce your
own milk, your own shoes, your own wagon, then you bought
them from someone you knew, or almost knew. Customers
were people who bought things from other people, not a con-
sumptive conglomerate whose loyalty needed to be courted.
If you liked or didn't like a purchase, it had about as much
impact as liking or not liking a sweater your mom knitted you.
Then came telephones, catalogs, lines of credit, and by the early
1920s, a group of department store owners began to popularize
a new idea: there was such thing as a customer, and that customer was always right. These entrepreneurs felt it important
to be accountable to their clientele, not because of any business
ethic, but because people were reluctant to open their wallets
for caveat emptor. The power of the almighty dollar rested in
their hands. So a contract was forged between seller and buyer:
if you give me money, I'll make sure you're satisfied.

But this contract proved fragile. Retailers were always
finding ways to wriggle out. A satisfaction guarantee seemed
reassuring until customers realized that only the extremely or
pathologically dissatisfied would go to the lengths required to
hold companies to their promise. Between you and satisfaction stood fine print and proofs of purchase, call centers and
interminable holds. More often than not, it wasn't an oven that
exploded or a bike that fell to pieces, but a can opener whose
blade dulled, a sock that wore through the heel, nothing worth
the trouble of a formal complaint, just a small thud of dissatis-

faction as another object quietly broke its promise. Every purchase was a trust fall.

Reviews injected a sense of justice into an otherwise faceless, powerless consumer experience. News articles heralded Epinions and Yelp for bringing democracy to online shopping, and indeed, by helping consumers make informed decisions, these sites had sanctified the wisdom of crowds. Good reviews became powerful, because satisfied customers could breed more satisfied customers. And if a customer was not satisfied, their bad review could turn the crowd's wisdom into a weapon.

In review culture, the power of the buyer is directly proportional to the power of the seller. If you suddenly decide you don't like your Target waffle iron, it will be replaced frictionlessly, even after months, even if the waffle iron didn't do anything wrong; you barely even need to speak to a person. Returning the waffle iron is like tossing an apple core on the forest floor, an act made harmless by the enormous, Godlike ecosystem that would happily swallow it up. The customer is not an individual, but part of a unified front, and so it's imperative that a company cede to their demands. Once, when I politely informed an agent that I'd been sent the wrong color tank top, he said he could *only imagine* how frustrated I must be, for it was *never his intention* to make me wait for my item, and he would do *all he could* to make things right. I felt like a baby tyrant. His obsequity shamed me. It reminded me that my power was weak because it had been granted to me, like mercy.

The more equal the power between buyer and seller, the more you must treat your interaction as a social one, bound by the usual social contracts, and thus the less deference the seller owes you. If the face oil you buy from a small business doesn't wow you, the money your dissatisfaction costs them is not a drop in the corporate bucket—it matters. And so they are loath to acquiesce to your demands, and you are loath to issue them. And if the TV you buy from some Craigslist guy breaks? Well, that's just the world. The guy is just a guy and so are you. He owes you nothing, and there is nobody to absorb the wrong but you. We call that bad luck.

Before review culture, when consumer grievances were attached to a person and not a corporation, the question of justice was tricky. My parents have never been the type to snap at the waiter, to leave a bad tip, or to send something back. Even when a complaint would be warranted, they usually stay quiet. Once, at a Tommy Bahama restaurant in Orlando, my dad found a jagged shard of steel in his coconut shrimp, but he said nothing to the staff, even at our urging. The idea that he could tell the waiter, summon the manager, then graciously accept their profuse apologies—this seemed too much of a fuss to be worth it. To present your bare anger to a stranger is intimidating for most people, but it is equally intimidating to temper that anger with the grace required to reach a resolution. Most people know what they want, but very few know how to ask for it. They know how to be enraged, and how to be pleased, but not the path between those two poles. It's the reason why the word *confront* is an aggression.

———

In Iowa, I once saw a neurologist for chronic disturbances that were either tiny seizures or tiny panic attacks. As I followed her to the exam room, she stopped and turned back to me. *Beach ball*, she said. I opened my mouth to say *Sure*. What was I agreeing to? *Red tulip*, she continued. *Chevrolet*. The words were a test, she explained. I'd be asked to recite them at the end of the appointment. Then, I told her about my problem.

I called them sneezes, after the mundane event that always marked their onset. The first one happened soon after I arrived in Iowa City for graduate school. I was three hours into an orientation session. I listened to a librarian talk about the first folio as I stared at the wall behind him, where there hung one of those commemorative quilts that seem to be made for no other purpose than to decorate the hallways of municipal buildings, when suddenly, quietly, my brain burst. An image came to me of a gold-sequined skirt attached to a girl, came like a fragment of a dream suddenly remembered. It felt like the Sunday after you drink too much, where your night comes back to you in queasy pieces. It felt like an attack of unconnected memories. I went to the bathroom and pressed my head against the wall.

In seconds, the feeling passed. But from then on, I'd get a sneeze a couple times a week. *Do you think the girl is you?* asked the neurologist. I said maybe, but I'd never owned such a skirt. She nodded, agreed to order me an EEG and a battery of neuropsychological assessments. Her tone was one of gentle curiosity, like my brain was a game she could play all day. Later, as we said goodbye in the waiting room, she asked me for the words, which I had been repeating obsessively in my head the whole time. *Beach ball, red tulip, uh*, I paused, *Corvette?*

Close, she said, smiling.

I liked the doctor in that moment. I kept apologizing to

her for the vagueness of my ailment, for potentially making
a fuss out of garden-variety anxiety, but she gave me permission to be concerned. The bad review came later, when all the
tests she'd ordered came back inconclusive and my insurance
company refused to cover them. *Your diagnostic code says temporary alteration of "awareness,"* the agent said on the phone, *and
we only cover a temporary alteration of "consciousness."* It was true
that I hadn't lost consciousness, but if you were conscious and
unaware, what kind of consciousness was that? I'd been healthy
and parentally insured my whole life, and in that comfortable
state, I'd forgotten that health care, too, was a transaction, that
medical procedures carried a price tag like anything else. When
I talked to the kind doctor, I was buying something. When
a nurse glued dozens of electrodes to my scalp, I was buying
that too. The ball, the tulip, the Chevrolet, all purchases. The
whole experience seemed orchestrated to make me forget this
fact, so when I walked out of the hospital having handed over
the $20 co-pay that felt more like an honorarium than a fee, I
thought that was the end of it, and that the real price tag would
stay hidden, like it usually did. But the doctor never returned
my calls asking her to appeal the denial, and so I navigated to
her review page while I stared, in tears, at the $3,000 medical
bill on the table next to me. As I looked at a review that said *I
wouldn't recommend her to a rat*, I began to calm down. Though
it had jarred me to remember that her care had merely been
a transaction, transaction was a language I spoke fluently. All
that made her beholden to my care was a flimsy code of eth-
ics, some wishy-washy paragraph whose terms were no more
enforceable than the Pledge of Allegiance. But a review would

behold her to my money, which she needed far more than my ethical regard. I was the customer, and I was still righteous.

In fact, reviews can make anything beholden to you, giving the power of transaction to every type of experience you can think of. It's not just movies and restaurants; it's your visit to the Statue of Liberty, your daily bus route, your acid trip. If someone does something bad, like kill a lion or be a racist, there is recourse far beyond quiet condemnation and gritted teeth. Now, you can punish them by flooding their bar or their dental practice with bad reviews, the one-star Yelp rating now a form of vigilante justice. Reviews have provided a pathway for social rage, though where the path leads remains unclear. As review culture spreads, it becomes harder to tame. Reviews have become our collective diary; the act of writing them, a confession. Someone's review of a pair of house slippers might reveal a constant, abiding pain. A review for a garden hose might seethe with anger. Before we can be Ems, we must be open wounds.

The most vicious review I've ever written was for a thing I didn't buy. During high school, my sense that I was smart and well-liked disintegrated. I couldn't study or play sports, couldn't charm teachers, couldn't understand physics, chemistry, or Japanese characters the way I had understood books, but even books I couldn't bring myself to read anymore. When the sentences glided over me as they always had, I felt not the pleasure of immersion but a frantic duty to grab them as they slid, pin them to meaning, pin the meaning to paper, and let the paper decide my fate. When boarding school kicked me out and I enrolled in a local one, my grades were still bad.

There, though, school was just school, not a holistic grooming experience that cost as much as a house, and adults didn't see my failures as a reflection of my character. Most of my teachers seemed either sympathetic to me or neutral, and so even when I got a C in a gym class called Mind and Body, even when I was suspended twice, the gestures felt numerical, not personal. Except for one.

Up until that point, I had found history to be a relatively safe subject, one that did not ask me to memorize or explicate so much as to observe and synthesize the facts of the world. But my history teacher was the kind who prides himself on the notoriety of his rigor and thus makes you fear an entire discipline for the rest of your life. In his hands, history became another test. Its tidal rhythms, the impressions they'd left on the rocks, these seemed to matter less than the names and dates we were to memorize for exams. Our textbooks rendered war and innovation and the rise and fall of empires in the same flat, fact-stuffed drone. The teacher dinged us for each fact that slid out of our brains. I could see his irritation mounting in the red-pen markings on my exams, which began as explanations and then reduced to *Really?*, *No*, and *X*. At the end of the semester, it became clear that I'd fail the class if I stayed in it. The school counselor gave me permission to switch from the AP section into a regular one, and she had me go sit in on a class. The regular classes were two rungs below the APs—they'd skipped me right past Honors. If you took the top two rungs, it was because you'd been told you were special, and if you took the regular classes, it was because, at some point, you and school had looked at each other and shrugged. It didn't matter who shrugged first. I'd been told I was smart my whole life, and still, here I was. In that class, the teacher had us study Bob Dylan lyrics, and she discussed the final project, which was to make a Myspace profile for a war criminal. In the AP class, my attention had been commanded, but here, it was courted, if crudely.

On the last day before winter break began, as my final AP history class came to a close, I joined the line of students that formed in front of my teacher's desk. I clutched the slip of paper that would make my transfer official. Until now, I'd kept my transfer a secret from my teacher, first out of shame, then out of defiance. He'd given me Ds all semester, and it was finally my turn to grade him back. I was rejecting him, his class, and his entire pedagogical apparatus.

I watched his face brighten as he laughed with the student in front of me, then slacken back to neutral as I approached his desk. I pushed the paper across the desk and said coolly, *Sign this*, tingling with anticipation. I'd rehearsed the scene in the shower that morning, assuming he'd take it as a personal referendum, perhaps plead with me or else lash out and list all the ways I was unfit for the class. But all he said was *Hm, you're sure?* and then *Happy holidays*. I'd imagined the grade he gave me to have been issued with an anger equal to the devastation it caused me, but it was just a number he'd typed into a box. I wanted his rage to reveal my failure as brave martyrdom, and his as puny captiousness. I wanted to be flayed flaw by flaw as I stood before him. I said *Happy holidays to you too*.

The minute I got home, I opened RateMyTeachers.com. I wrote my review in a fury, noting that his eyeglasses were Prada

but he still looked like a pedophile, that he got off on the fear
and adoration of sixteen-year-olds. The review has since been
removed by the site, probably for being egregiously personal.
I might have taken a jab at his baby, I don't remember. In that
moment, I was Emily, not Em, and my review was not a review
but a scream in a hot, dark room.

But that review had been years ago, and I'd changed. Em
would never have allowed it. Once, Emily entered an expensive salon asking for a lived-in lob, but as she explained what
she wanted to the stylist, she sensed that the woman wasn't
listening, that her nods and mhms were inattention masquer-
ading as recognition, and so, an hour later, Emily exited the
salon with an abominable wedge for which she'd still tipped
25 percent. As Emily seethed in her car, she had the urge to
open Yelp right then and there, to pen a screed about how the
stylist seemed stoned and dim, and the salon was delusional to
charge those prices in a town like this. How she wished she'd
gone to a real city where people knew what they were doing,
where the expensive shampoo didn't smell like cheap air fresh-
ener. But Em told her to wait. So Emily rubbed her foul little
undercut, and Em waited. Emily cried counting the months it
would take to look normal again. Still, Em waited. Em waited
until Emily's anger had cooled into reason. And then, Em set
to her task. Em's review didn't attack the stylist who did it.
Em didn't even name her. She simply posted the photos and
described what happened, just like she posted photos of IKEA
shelves damaged in transit and captioned them *Disappointed*. If
Emily touched the bare flame of experience, then Em was its
cold, knowing arbiter.

Recently, I came across a start-up called Empathiq, which offers a "review concierge" service for health-care providers. Empathiq aggregates patient reviews across seventy-plus health review sites, crunches the numbers, and tells doctors how to improve their practice. They insist that a single review on a site like Yelp or Google can affect a practitioner's annual income by as much as 10 percent. I paused for a moment at this figure, thinking of the review I'd given the history teacher. A few years later, he'd resigned amid mounting student complaints. It was the same gripes I'd had about him: he harped on trivial details, he played favorites. My anger long cooled, I now felt guilty, wondering whether his performance review had included my own. I thought of the two-star reviews Em had given to the doctor and the hair salon. For years, long after the cut had grown out and my devastation had shrunk into a party anec-dote, women would message me on Yelp asking for the name of the stylist who'd given me the terrible haircut, fearing the same thing would happen to them, and I would divulge it, and so they'd go to someone else. Em hadn't named the stylist in her review because she wasn't the kind of reviewer who sought revenge, but here Emily was, naming her anyway. But naming her was just the truth, not retribution. If truth could be warped by passion and fury, then justice was the absence of both.

Em's truths were powerful, though. Word-of-mouth mar-keting has long been considered the most potent form of advertising, but before review culture, it usually came from mouths that you knew. Though online reviews are written by strangers, they enjoy that same sense of trust, because we tend to give the most trust to the people who need it the least. It's why *I have nothing to gain* is an assertion of honesty. After MakeupAlley came the YouTube beauty influencers, who were not yet called influencers, but *gurus*, which reflected their power as wise and benevolent teachers. The gurus on YouTube were shinier, more enthusiastic than the girls in the Alley; they liked most things they tried, which sanctified my urge to buy them, and besides, Sephora and Ulta now had their own review feature right there below the product page. I spent less and less time in the Alley.

But as companies caught wind of their power as word-of-mouth advertisers, gurus and reviewers began to carry a familiar stench. After all, a middling three-star average could kill a product, while a single viral post in praise of it could crash websites and rattle supply chains. Influenster, a company that sends consumers free products in exchange for reviews, provides a style guide that includes tenets like *Go Bare*, *Say It Don't Sell It*, *Cut Out the Bias*, and *Innovation Not Imitation*, which implies that even reviews for Greek yogurt and press-on nails are not safe from the scourge of plagiarism. The Sephora reviewers began to sound suspicious: every product had a four-star average, every other reviewer had been sent the product for free. There were even whispers that the site mysteriously 404'd when users tried to post a negative review, and the negative ones that did get published were buried by the algorithm far beneath the raves. I met someone at a party who said she'd been offered ten dollars a pop to write fake reviews for things she'd never even touched; in fact, entire websites sprang up to tell consumers what percentage of a product's reviews were fake—often, it was more than half. Lies, like ads, grew where money did. When I desperately returned to MakeupAlley seeking honest reviews, it had become a ghost town.

Yelp stayed active, but it had become unusable. Anytime I considered a new bar or restaurant, even if I was standing right in front of it, I'd dutifully open the app, squinting down at my little screen to determine whether the experience was worth having, in my head the cloud of witnesses who'd done me the favor of having it for me. But rarely did my experience match the aggregated rating on the restaurant's Yelp page, which somehow always seemed to be four stars. Many people gave five stars indiscriminately, an ethos that reflected two things: first, that people don't care about the same things in the same amounts, and second, that while a three-star review is technically average, it's actually punitive and everyone knows it. In the grad school orientation where I'd felt my first sneeze, the head of the teaching-assistant program had attempted the same argument when she informed us that we were supposed to give 40 percent of our students C grades, and I balked just as Yelp reviewers did, because reviews, like college grades, had become so high-stakes, so freighted with the fate of someone else's livelihood, that to give a true assessment felt unjust. The one-star reviews that peppered each Yelp page felt no truer than the five-stars, filled as they were with petty grievances, furious blocks of text, vows of revenge. Approval and condemnation were equally unreliable, their extremes canceling each other out.

What's more, people had started to review *me*. One man whose tiny Tucson guesthouse I'd rented on Airbnb tore into me for leaving crumbs in the bed. He began his review, *Emily and her girlfriend seem like nice people . . .* I obsessed over the rating I'd received as an Uber passenger, which was two-tenths short of a perfect five. And then there were course evaluations, which my students filled out each semester. One girl with a pinched mouth was furious about her final grade even after I'd bumped it from a B to a B+. She sneered that I wore see-through shirts and occasionally had hickeys on my neck, and she wasn't even lying, I was a slut in those years. *As an education major,* she wrote, *I hope to never be as horrible a teacher as Emily.* From then on, I brought my students doughnuts and feared their every eye roll. When a kiosk in an airport bathroom asked me to rate the cleanliness of the facilities, I stood there jabbing the smiley face over and over again. The girl's review rang in my ears.

I began to long for a time before reviews, a time when getting a slice of pizza or buying new body wash was a task as uncomplicated as mailing a letter or clipping a toenail. Once, I could just sniff a bottle at the drugstore and buy it because it smelled like oranges. Now, I obsessively read product reviews for anything I even considered buying, becoming an expert in nonstick grill pans or toothbrush holders or magnetic refrigerator notepads. I wanted the best, the most aesthetically pleasing, the artisanal, the special, and so the orange-scented body wash had been replaced by chains of search terms in endless permutations of scent, texture, packaging, price, and size. The orange-scented body wash splintered into *Neroli shower gel pump price low to high* and *Mandarin sulfate free shea wash* and *Bergamot moisturizing cream oil 8 oz.* The ostensible purpose of the product had always been simple: to clean me. If all I wanted was to be clean, I could drive ten minutes to Target. But I'd tried that before. The whole thing broke down in the aisle. The permutations I'd once controlled with fingers and search terms now filled my field of vision, all at once. There was no way to know which one was the best. I could realize that there was a limit to how clean I could get, a limit to the pleasure I could derive from the smell of citrus, and just grab anything. Or I could open the bottles and hold them close to my nose, rub the gel between my fingers. Instead, I crouched in the aisle and clawed for cell service, I who was afraid to buy anything without witnesses, I who appended the word *Wirecutter* to every search, from scissors to dustpans. Even if the reviews were true, what fate were they delivering me from? In my attempts to reduce the friction between me and certain objects, I'd multiplied the frictions that inevitably remained. If I believed there was a best body wash, I had to fear the worst. If I had a god, I needed a devil. Back in the Target aisle, I couldn't get any bars. I stood up and left the store with no body wash. It took me one more week and three more collective hours to choose a new one.

The last Yelp review I ever wrote was three stars for a burrito that had failed me in triplicate: it took an hour to make, was inedible, and somehow still cost twenty dollars. I was annoyed. But like all my reviews, this one was exceedingly fair, mild even. I was sympathetic to how overworked the kitchen must be, how expensive food had become, but I concluded that these prices still seemed high, that the manager should hire more people. I felt satisfied with my feedback until the restaurant owner responded to me, sending me a private message on Yelp. *Hi Emily*, he began, though Em was the name I'd listed. He went on to say that the restaurant had to pay $15,000 a month in Grubhub fees, that inflation had driven prices up and the place had barely broken even in the past four years. *Still*, he continued, *all that matters is the customer's perception of value. So, I'm going to continue to re-evaluate our choices.* I navigated to the review I'd written, read it over again. My words had been true. They'd been, I thought, just. I'd spoken and he'd listened, I'd evaluated and he'd evaluated. Weren't we now moving, together, toward change? Faced with the product of my constructive criticism, I couldn't now say what I'd been trying to construct. I felt spotlit and chastened. And then, though the owner hadn't asked me to, I deleted the review. I opened my review of the hair salon. I deleted it too. I deleted two- and three-star reviews of an ice cream shop in my college town, a salad place near the Ulta where I'd worked, a boutique in Iowa City that sold stupid little succulents. I clicked until I'd deleted them all. I haven't written one since. The urge still comes sometimes when I'm irritated, and I'll open the app and begin to compose one. I'll move clauses around and search for the right turns of phrase and hover, when I'm finished, above the Publish button, but I never click it. The review gets swallowed into the trash folder like so many other wounded text messages never meant to be read.

Finally, here it was. The wisdom of crowds hadn't been impenetrable to tyranny and apathy, and the algae of advertising I thought I'd shaken off had simply grown back in new forms. Laws were enacted that forced gurus and reviewers to disclose when their opinions had, in fact, been purchased, but in between these paid ads were the demented cousins of ads: affiliate links, clicks and likes, elaborate fruit baskets with handwritten notes. When the influencers wanted to post about a product that they hadn't been paid to promote, they would fervently assert *This is not an ad, This is not an ad, This is not an ad, I just like it.* When I opened Yelp to write a review, I told myself *This is just the truth, This is just the truth, This is just the truth, I'm not lying.* I'd told myself that the reviews had been true, but they hadn't really. They had never been testimony, or if they had been testimony, then testimony didn't promise justice. Testimony didn't really have a point at all, because it had always been just more words from a mouth. It was unclear which was more unsettling: that we might all be consciously lying, that we might be lying without knowing, or that we might be telling the truth and were pleading with everyone else, our mouths full of worms, to believe us this time.

I believed that reviews empowered me to make the best choices, and with them I could empower others to do the same. There was a best and we'd find it, there was a perfect and it waited for us, there was a dupe somewhere laughing, there was a truth and a way and false idols needed to be cast aside until we found the products that would save us, our Kingdoms on Earth. Reviews were a blade of truth that sliced through the dark consumer jungle. But I always ended up back in the undergrowth. I thought a review was like pinching yourself awake in the middle of a nightmare. But maybe it was like telling yourself, in the middle of the nightmare, *I'm dreaming*, but you still can't wake up.

While Supplies Last

I WON A YEAR'S SUPPLY of LaCroix in the summer of 2017. Everyone I know loves LaCroix, not just the drink, but what it means to drink it, the limber, eccentric, and vaguely French affinity group to which their beverage choice aligns them. The contest was sponsored by a local grocery store, and when they announced my win across their social media accounts, everyone seemed a little jealous. Strangers messaged me things like *That should have been mine* or *Can I have a case?* Coworkers popped their heads into my cubicle to congratulate me, having seen the announcement on their Facebook feeds because they had entered the contest too.

My summers had never been bikes, tans, freedom. They were the wrong kind of hot and wet. Clean sweat is active, muscular, beads neatly on skin like in a Gatorade commercial. Dirty sweat seeps viscous from armpit and crotch and back of neck, supine, couchbound. Clean sweat smells like saltwater. Dirty sweat smells like stew. My small private grade school was in the next suburb over, too far to walk or bike, and so were all my friends. High school and college were in entirely different states. School was always where my real life was, so time and narrative slackened each June. My summers were stew.

In May of 2016, when my first year of graduate school ended and my teaching stipend along with it, my girlfriend Kylie and I began selling plasma. I felt like I had to do it, though looking back, I'm not sure why. My parents gave me generous checks for Christmas, birthdays, and sometimes, as I left to go to the airport, my dad would press a handful of twenties into my palms. I felt genuine worry every time my bank account got down to double digits, but the swaddle of wealth hovered always nearby. My parents could buy my entire life. They could buy it and go about their day. They could buy my dream and have several dreams to spare. Inside their American dream they could fit the whole of my friends' dreams, and their parents' dreams, and their parents' parents' dreams. I feared being broke the way you fear death in a video game.

But that was last summer. In the summer of LaCroix, I had a real job. Every morning I'd wake up and drive ten minutes to an office complex, where I wrote passages for standardized tests. They were about things like pioneering female scientists or a certain species of tree frog, the kind of educational pabulum that is by necessity so neutrally voiced, so ethically placid, that if you didn't know better, you might assume it was written by a hyperliterate machine, not an affable human being with a master's degree. We had to inform without provoking. We had to be frank but gentle with subjects that implied the existence of poverty or racism. We could write about climate change, as long as we did not suggest that it was directly caused by humans. It made the pieces surprisingly difficult to write and, at times, frustrated everyone, but we knew that to present young test-takers with the world as they actually understood it, charged and fractured and dissonant, was to do them a disservice. If a subject might pull a student out of the test and into a sore awareness of the real world, it was flagged with the word *touchy*.

That summer, I was making more money than I'd ever made in my life. Had my internship turned into a full-time job, my yearly pay would've been $40,000, and this felt like a lavish sum. And so, that summer, I shopped with a vigor that startled even me.

If I was awake and not on the clock, I was on my phone, and if I was on my phone, I was building a cart. At first, I did this on my phone's web browser, typing in the *S* for Sephora, or the *E* for eBay, but eventually this became too tedious. Once, I'd drawn a line that had kept me from downloading dedicated store apps, but that line had been stretching for months, first to the CVS app, then the one for Target, and finally to the McDonald's app, after which the line dissolved completely. By mid-June, my shopping apps sat in a dedicated folder on my phone that I marked with the winged money emoji. I had Etsy and Taco Bell and Forever 21. I had Nordstrom and Papa John's and Gap. I'd find someplace to sit or sprawl and open each one up like a portal to a new world, my body still but for a few fingers, which manipulated the screen with the tender and knowing finesse of a carpenter, or a brain surgeon. With only my thumb I could open up the new arrivals and re-sort them price low-high, I could add three different things to my cart and then flip among them, reading the reviews of each. Collectively, shopping ate up the bulk of my waking life. But each small step of the ritual felt effortless, took me seconds. It was muscle memory.

Shopping was, in fact, the only thing I did with vigor. This was my first office job, and I initially assumed that if I found it numbing, it was because the office was, itself, dead, a place with boring people and bad coffee that conspired to slowly suck the life out of you. This, I had heard, is what offices were like. I was surprised to find that what flattened my brain was not my coworkers, who were funny and intelligent, or the coffee, which was decent when I got there and became even better when they switched to a newer, fancier brewing system. It wasn't a lack of leisure time, for I still had plenty of that. The numbness was not caused by my desk, which I could raise and lower at the push of a button, nor by the room I worked in, which at least had a sunny window overlooking the parking lot, nor even by the work itself, which was gratifying in the way math problems can be. It was me. Every summer of my life had felt heavy and dull, but I hadn't noticed it as a pattern until my twenty-sixth go at it. Before, each June, I would eagerly anticipate a sunwashed montage. Three months later, I would sit on the edge of September and conclude that this summer had just been a fluke, a weird one, and it was time, now, to rebloom into autumn. I preferred to assume that my sluggishness set in because I had no routine, no car, no friends nearby. But now that I had all three, the extraordinary sameness of my office routine simply acted as a control for all other factors, allowing me to observe the interior shifts that would usually be swallowed up by the chaos of everyday life. My day-to-day activities were like hospital food. They provoked nothing in me, and in that nothing, I could notice things.

School was routine, camp was routine, but nothing had been quite so regular as this. I was sitting in the same exact room every single day for the same exact amount of time, with no real responsibilities or distractions besides. Save for occasional intrusions by, say, the sun, or a conversation, my life was a rotating series of seats and screens: phone in bed, phone on walk to desk, Lenovo ThinkPad at desk, phone on office toilet, mirror, car, windshield, phone in parked car outside my house for half an hour before remembering to go inside to use the bathroom, if peeing OK to hold phone, if shitting grudgingly set it down, then undress, resume phone in bed, TV, phone during TV, phone and my face the only glow in a dark room until finally, sleep, closed eyes, a dark room. Some people are dogged by a rabbit-eyed inability to sit still, others a punishing, consuming melancholy, but my brain chemistry, I realized, felt like a chronic, mild flu, my body like a spoon dragged through honey. At the end of each day, my step count rarely exceeded three digits, and I still felt exhausted.

Besides shopping, my hobby was entering contests. Or, not contests—that implies a competition of skill. I began entering sweepstakes. I sought and entered them en masse, methodically clicking through a long list of links as I lay in bed, chin to chest, phone growing hotter and hotter in its rubber case until it would issue a temperature warning and force me to lay it down to cool off.

There were so many sweepstakes to enter. Some asked me to submit, along with my contact info, my favorite thing about their product, like organic milk or Rain-X windshield wipers, and so I'd debase myself with a little sentence, like *Tastes great in cereal and coffee!* or *Wipes away rain effectively!* Some asked me to spin wheels or pull a lever or play a brief matching game. Those I loved. Some asked me to submit a recipe, or post a picture, and those were ignored. Some needed only my email.

Then there was the matter of the spoils. They ranged from the practical to the insulting. For every $1,000 Visa gift card, there were just as many coupons for a free jar of vitamin gummies. Sometimes I could win an experience, like dinner in Paris or a glamping trip with Oprah, but I entered those with the knowledge that you can usually exchange an experience for its equivalent cash value, which is what I intended to choose. I was in no fit state to meet Oprah.

I was obsessed with the idea of winning, and at some point that summer, I became equally interested in what happened *after* a big win. I found a subreddit of people who had won large supplies—month, year, lifetime—of a single thing. The definition and delivery of these amounts is up to the company's discretion, and no two were alike. Some people got everything all at once—a pallet with a thousand bars of soap, or enough boxes of Apple Jacks to feed an entire neighborhood for a month. These were the kinds of stories I savored. Cartoonish and satisfying. Others got their prize in installments, like the guy who received a case of Mars bars every month. For some lifetime winners, the installments never stopped, following them into new eras, a marker of elapsed time as perennial as the seasons. Somebody said their cousin won a lifetime supply of Rice-A-Roni at age twelve, and she still, at age twenty-eight, received a case in the mail at the beginning of each year. Some prizes defined the span of a life stingily—one winner's "lifetime supply" of high-quality knives amounted to only two because, the company insisted, just one should last you a lifetime. A lot of people received something disappointingly immaterial, like 365 individual coupons for a free bag of Skittles.

I won the LaCroix in July. It was the first time, and so far the last, that anything had ever come of my sweepstaking. A lot of people said *congratulations*. I'd always thought *congratulations* was meant to praise someone for something they'd earned, a synonym for *good job*. On my phone, I looked it up, and it turns out I was wrong. Congratulations means not necessarily that you've done the good thing, just that one has happened to you. But to me, the distinction did not seem trivial.

I went with Kylie to pick the boxes up on a Saturday. We helped the store's manager wheel the cases to my car on a flat-bed cart. On his phone, he snapped a photo of me standing next to my prize for the store's Facebook page, my arm curled around the open trunk as if it held a buck I'd just killed. We thanked the manager and drove home, the little Honda lurching under the weight of 432 cans.

I should mention that I hate LaCroix. I hated it before I entered the contest, and I hated it after. Every time I cracked open a LaCroix at a party, I was shocked by the tenacity of its blandness. The cultish devotion of its drinkers annoyed me even more. How could anyone love canned seltzer that much, let alone make it a part of their identity? Why did the company insist on an incorrect pronunciation of the name, and why did this somehow feel more snobbish, not less, than the proper French? And why, still, did I feel embarrassed for hating it? Why did my no-calorie drinks of choice have to be the sad,

demented cousins of soda, like Diet Dr.Pepper and Sugar-Free
Red Bull and Gatorade Zero? Why did each can of LaCroix
proclaim *Innocent!* and why, when I'd lucked into hundreds of
them, did I feel so guilty? I couldn't explain the thought process that led me to enter. Did I imagine I'd gift it to my friends
who loved the drink? Did I hope that winning might make
me love it too? I'd asked for something I didn't really want
and received it in enormous quantities. My dazed and roving
thumb had led me here.

Somewhere in between the eighteen trips it took to haul
the cases from the car to the front door in 90-degree heat,
Kylie and I became annoyed, whether at the task or at each
other, I can't remember. She stopped making trips to the car,
and I carried in the last several cases myself, damp and per-
turbed. I stood panting in the small kitchen. The cases had
overtaken it. A tower of Passion Fruits reached from the floor
to the light switch. Two cases of Tangerine stood on top of the
microwave, and two more on the windowsill behind the sink.

What should we do now, I said, less a question than a statement of being alive. You do one thing, then you do another.

In those months, Kylie and I struggled to find reasons to
get out of bed. At the beginning of our relationship, it was a
haven. Kylie was not a bed person by nature, but I showed her
how it could be a kingdom. We filled entire days with cuddling
and sex, TV marathons, expansive talks as we propped our heads
up on one elbow, our faces only inches apart. Over time, we
forgot the house had other surfaces. I felt as if I'd infected her
with a disease. We ate in bed, we scrolled through our phones in
bed, and if the food we were making was going to take fifteen

minutes in the oven, we'd lie in bed to wait for it. We made carts in our bed, wordlessly texting each other multipacks of beef jerky. Very rarely did we fuck in our bed. If we left, the reason was usually hunger. We'd get in my car and drive to the grocery store, standing in front of the hot bar like new parents peering into a hospital nursery, or to the Arby's drive-through line, placing our orders and then impulsively adding one last additional item for fear that we'd never be full. Sometimes we'd go to Walmart for absolutely nothing at all. Other times CVS or Walgreens. But most often, we went to the same place every other American goes when they want a roof for boredom, a place to shuffle around in the company of others.

What should we do, I repeated. Kylie paused, then flatly suggested what we'd been doing all summer: the mall.

We set out for Coral Ridge under a slowly greening sky, the air a swollen belly of vapor. By the time we reached the highway, rain had started to fall, and when we pulled up to the mall a few minutes later, it was pounding. We ran across the parking lot, and by the time we reached the atrium, we were soaked. Stepping through the glass doors, we immediately felt the blast of industrial air-conditioning and began to shiver. Somewhere between the main doors and the Chick-fil-A, our tension from earlier turned into a fight. It wasn't the kind where heat is transferred back and forth in the form of words, but the kind where it dies in silence. We said almost nothing.

Outside, the sky had gone teal. Kylie paced along the food court, surveying her options, as I sat down to watch people loop around the ice rink, which was open year-round. At that moment, an alarm began to blare throughout the mall. Different from the monotone chirp of a fire alarm, an indoor tornado alarm sounds like a siren; not the long, undulating wail of an ambulance, which vaguely approaches a tune, but a clipped version that is doomed to climb, stop short, and climb again incessantly, until the danger has passed. The tornado watch for our county had become a tornado warning, and a prerecorded male voice told us to immediately seek shelter in one of the designated safety areas. His message and the alarm rang out across the food court on a loop. A few people shuffled noncommittally to the shelter area. Several people, shopping bags in hand, walked out the doors and into the parking lot, where it was now hailing. Most people did nothing at all. After fifteen minutes or so, some of the food court workers retreated back into the kitchens, which I guess were their safe areas, but one pizza restaurant, whether out of capitalistic devotion or simple inertia, stayed open, and a long line formed in front of it. Kylie returned to my table, where I hadn't moved. The alarm was still blaring.

She asked if I wanted anything. I glanced at her, then stared at a nearby security guard who was, for some reason, dragging the heavy mall-grade triple-barrel garbage cans into the middle of the floor. I said nothing. She walked away.

A few weeks earlier, a friend had come to visit me in Iowa City. Visitors have a way of laying your entire life bare for you. Take away work, and suddenly, you have shapeless days that must be filled with activity. First, you plan to visit your favorite restaurants and bars, but then you need to find things to do between eating and drinking. You're forced to ask the question *What do I do for fun?* Maybe you google *Things to do in X*, X being your home. You find yourself suggesting things that sound like a middle school date. A museum. The mall. The movies. A walk in the park. What you want to do with your friend is exist, but you must orchestrate a series of distractions that turn existing into an activity. You do one thing, then you have to do another.

It took an hour to show my friend downtown Iowa City. We were excited to see each other after a long time apart, and spent the whole time talking, barely catching our breath. Kylie and I were like that once too, but our time in bed had rendered us mute. Now, here was a friend, fresh air, and the words spilled out. Occasionally I'd interrupt our conversation to point out a landmark. Here was a restaurant I liked. Here was the ugly building by the river where I taught and took classes. Here were some little boutiques, a frozen yogurt place, undergraduates in lanyards and athletic shorts, open patches of grass. After that, we went to one of the restaurants I'd pointed out, where we sat on chairs and talked, and then to a bar, where we talked in a booth. On the second day, we went to another restaurant, and didn't want to go to a bar. The third day we spent on my couch, and we were running out of things to talk about. Had she stayed a fourth day, we probably would have just lain in our separate beds the whole time, looking at our phones. On the fifth day, the mall would have called.

———

Kylie had finished her food. The alarm was still blaring and the sky was nearly black. It was clear now that we couldn't leave. I asked if we should take cover. Kylie asked if we should stay still. We left each other's questions hanging in the air. All summer, the architecture of our contentment had been so fragile that it could be shattered by a look, a gesture. Our fights were just as fragile—I recognized that this moment could be a way out. A look or a gesture could shatter the tension, if only for the next few hours. All I had to do was soften. But the architecture of loathing was robust. It was such an easy landmark, a place in which any unfocused pain could seek shelter. Like the mall, it was a place our boredom could return to. And so all I said, in the flattest voice I could muster, was *Let's just walk.*

We walked down the tiled promenade, the skylights above us now lightless and lashed with rain and hail. The mall had opened in 1998, and Kylie had grown up an hour away from it, so each time we went, she'd list all the ways it used to be better. We passed the empty storefront that was once a Gap, the cell phone kiosk that used to sell little scented soaps. Because of the storm, all the stores were now shuttered. The kiosks were cloaked in black vinyl coverlets. The scent of Mahogany Teakwood three-wick candles seeped through the metal gate that had been pulled down over the Bath & Body Works.

The Sears that anchored the mall's northwest quadrant had been torn down a few years earlier. Stand-alone big-box stores with stand-alone entrances were being added in its place. There was a brand-new PetSmart, a Marshalls, and an Ulta. A Five Below and a HomeGoods were set to open in September. We walked to the south side of the mall and sat down on the floor in front of the former Younkers. In its place was a Spirit Halloween that at the tail end of every summer would crawl into the carcass of a closed store like a cockroach after a nuclear blast. Before Younkers, it had made its nest inside Sears. A few years later, I learned it was occupying the former Pier 1 Imports over by the Red Lobster.

Malls were dying, that's what everyone kept saying. I was part of a Facebook group called Dead Mall Enthusiasts, where people who had come of age during the heyday of mall culture would pen nostalgic odes to the malls of their youth, posting photos of empty storefronts and ghostly promenades. Sometimes, they would report on crimes in these dying malls, like the murder of a girl whose body decomposed for weeks in the back room of a food court in Atlanta, during what should've been a busy Christmas rush, but wasn't, because the mall saw so little foot traffic that it was practically abandoned. American shopping habits had veered away from the leisurely mall-cruising of the '80s and '90s and into the brusque, direct, big-box-friendly model of *pick a store and get out*. Online shopping was an extension of this ethos: Why amble when you can just buy? Malls were once our public square. Now, they were rotting.

Except here Kylie and I were, mall walkers. Here were the stores, surviving. I kept wanting to call Coral Ridge a dead mall, but a mall's deadness is measured by its vacancy rate, and Coral Ridge Mall wasn't *dying* (40 percent vacant), *unhealthy* (20 to 40 percent), or even *in trouble* (10 percent). Families still clustered here. The Easter Bunny still came. Going to the mall was something we all did, just like going to work, or scrolling in bed. A day was a vessel filled with something to do. So I did one thing, then I did another. My life had always been this. Why did I call this rotting?

———

The suburbs are a place with no center. The architect Victor Gruen hated them, primarily because they were hostile to ambling. Suburban residents had nowhere to flock, nowhere to

gather, just houses and strip malls and roads to take you there
and back. They were miles of private property dotted with per-
functory strips of green. So Gruen invented the modern American shopping mall. Gruen saw, in malls, a way to recreate the
European pedestrian square for an increasingly automobiled and
atomized populace. He envisioned that malls would blossom into
walkable downtowns with apartments, schools, hospitals. But in
the end, all that stuck were the stores. *I refuse to pay alimony to these
bastard developments*, he said, disowning them once and for all.

The thing is, malls did actually function, for decades, as
the thriving town squares he envisioned. Or at least, people
flocked to them. Thirty years ago, you might have walked into
the mall on a Saturday afternoon and stayed for hours. You'd
stroll the halls and peer into store windows. You'd see people
you knew with their friends or families, strangers relaxing on
pleather stools, children sitting with Santa Claus, children sitting with the Easter Bunny, teenagers leaning against glass rail-
ings, groups of seniors getting their steps in. My friend Daisy
recently visited Budapest, where American culture is a more
recent import: only when communism fell were our malls and
fast-food chains allowed to flow in. The city was on America's
timeline, she told me, but decades behind. Indoor malls were
bustling like it was the '80s. Every McDonald's was immaculate.
In Budapest, she marveled, *the most beautiful women you've ever
seen in your life are eating inside the KFC.*

When a professor of mine visited her grandparents' home
country and set foot on its soil, she said, she felt like her DNA
was singing. Every suburb is my hometown, every mall my lin-
eage. There's a mall in Boston that I go to only when someone

on my mom's side dies. It fills the baggy hours between the hotel check-in and the wake, between burial and dinner. There's a mall in Indiana where I lost my favorite stuffed duck, and a mall in New Hampshire where I first tried avocado. I've kissed girls inside the Lids store at the Mall of America, beneath the cloud-painted ceilings at the Forum in Las Vegas, sharing Häagen-Dazs at New Jersey's American Dream. I can navigate any mall as if by sonar. Small shifts in light and echo tell me a food court or an exit is near. Though the scent now makes me nauseous, I can sniff out Warm Vanilla Sugar across two city blocks. There's a Bath & Body Works at the Atlantic Terminal in the middle of Brooklyn and on the way to the train once, I found myself darting in. Before I could form a coherent narrative of what I was doing, I sprayed two pumps, and darted back out. I spent the rest of the day confused and scrubbing at my wrists.

Years after I'd left Iowa, I took a friend home with me for the holidays. We went to see a movie at one of my childhood malls. Afterward, we had time to kill before meeting my parents for dinner. Wandering around a mall was novel to her, a city kid who'd never even drunk a Coca-Cola, not out of virulent opposition, but out of the same ambivalence that has kept me from seeing an Avengers movie. Soda, like the mall, just wasn't in her vernacular. But I slipped into it like a warm bath. We shared pillowy bites from an Auntie Anne's pretzel as we flicked hangers along the racks. We took pictures of ourselves in funny hats. We held candles to our noses and took a deep breath. We had nowhere to be, we could go anywhere, and everywhere was having a sale. But as we wandered from the H&M to the Sephora to the Express, a familiar feeling began to seep in. My limbs were getting heavy, my mouth dry, and my eyes kept sliding around. Each store's particular arrangement of sound and light and temperature and scent had been calibrated with military-grade precision to coax my eyes to a shelf, my feet to a register, my fingers into my wallet. I began to feel like I was in a terrarium. Everything I saw had been strategically placed. Were the rocks rocks? Was the wood wood? Were the plants plants? The fake ones are so good now, you'd hardly tell the difference. A mini-train chugged around Santa's Village. We sat quietly on a bench, and I pressed my forehead to a cup of ice water from Sbarro. I had lingered there too long, my enthusiasm burning down like a wick. I knew exactly what was happening, yet it always took me by surprise. Sometimes it took an hour, sometimes three, but it always struck me, without fail. I'd never left a mall simply because I was satisfied. I was mall sad again.

Many people would call this suburban malaise. So commonly is suburbia described as a cultivar of hollow, stultifying sameness that the observation is now almost as ticky-tacky as suburbia itself, and it's hard to believe there was ever a time when suburbia was just a word, like *city* or *town* or *country*. Most people would say that shopping malls are sad for the same reason suburbs are sad. If leisure time is meant to be the opposite of work, then a Saturday spent cruising the mall could never grant reprieve from the isolating, exploitative drudgery of the American work-week because the mall, like the suburbs, has been constructed by these very same forces. Malls, like suburbs, sanction ambling only in service of capital. You walk with a sense of purpose singular enough to get you in the door, loose enough to allow for digression. From the moment you step through the doors of a mall, its serpentine layout tries to make you forget what you came for. In your disorientation, you buy more than you meant to. The bamboozlement even has a name: *the Gruen transfer.*

I was in the suburbs, and I felt malaise. Did suburbia cause the malaise? Or did my extant malaise find a home in suburbia? Sitting on the mall bench the evening before, I was sure it was the former. I thought *Yes, the mall has done this, the suburbs have done this, car culture and a cushy life of sameness has done this, Panera's Sierra Turkey sandwich with a side cup of soup has done this.* I looked around at the other mallgoers, and it didn't matter whether they felt bad themselves, because I felt bad for them. I couldn't imagine being happy in this place. It was the same pang I feel when I see an old man eating chili alone inside a Wendy's, or a child crying in an amusement park gift shop, or a pair of Skechers Shape-Ups. It's the kind of sadness that is rooted in pity. It makes you loathe yourself, because what right do you have to pity these people, you who are mean and weak, you whose frailty is worse because it is brittle.

The next day, my friend and I drove into Chicago and spent the day walking up and down a charming street lined with little cafés and shops, none of them chains but all of them somewhat replicable. I could see the aesthetic pleasure we both took in the scene, a relief from yesterday. But the pleasure annoyed me. Was the sadness I'd believed to be a deep-rooted sensitivity to the forces of capitalism simply a quibble over aesthetics? We passed yet another place with French fries in little silver cones and I thought, *Is this not just a Chili's?* I swept my hand along the row of stores and asked her a question I'd continue to ask when we returned to New York, on Fifth Avenue, on Vanderbilt, on so many charming little streets: *Is this not just a mall?*

The difference between a mall and Fifth Avenue is that Fifth Avenue can't provide shelter from a tornado. Fifth Avenue is porous to the ebb and flow of water, wind, heat, and people in a way malls are not. Fifth Avenue may be manicured and policed, but it is still possible to stage a protest outside a Louis Vuitton or sleep in its vestibule after hours. Rain can fall on your face, the smell of garbage can fill your nostrils, and you can stumble in by chance, on your way to somewhere else. Even when the mall is open to the public, it's sealed like a tomb. Malls masquerade as public squares, but every inch of them is private property, even the air. Cities are high-stakes video games where friction makes everything a quest, even ambling. We call the suburbs numbing because they are the same, frictionless, but in fact, friction is far more numbing. When we glide into an extraordinary sameness, we can begin to fully account for the material of our lives. We can begin to isolate. Then a new numbness is added. Then a new hunger. When you ask for ease, comfort, and stability and receive it in enormous quantities, you are then left to wonder whether you even wanted it in the first place. Then you must find new things to want.

Months later, I walked with friends down a street in Brooklyn. It was the first warm Saturday in March, the one where everyone spills out onto the streets with their jackets tied around their waists, finally believing what their minds have known to be true but their bodies refuse to accept without proof: that this time, too, winter will end. We sipped coffees, stopped in a bookstore, strolled through a sea of faces in the park and sat down on a bench to eat fresh fruit and sandwiches, alive and not a bit alone, doing all the things that are supposed to make life worth living in a bustling, walkable city. Then the mall feeling began slipping in. This warm, sweet day was not yet over, and I would have more that were exactly like this one, with coffee and parks and sandwiches and fruit, and between this day and those, there was time to fill. And if the sweet time was replicable, then so was the gray time and the flat time. How could I have thought this way of life superior? My urban malaise was simply suburban malaise sans pity, and beneath it was a constitutional discontent that I would always return to, no matter where I lived. My nightstand would fill up again with empty Diet Dr. Peppers, and then something would lift, and again, I'd clear them away. Something would have to take their place. I'd walk half the mall happy and half the mall sad. I did this thing, then I'd have to do another.

━━━

Finally, after Kylie and I had walked for an hour through the Coral Ridge Mall, the sirens stopped. The sun had set underneath the tornado, and now it was dark. We walked across the glistening parking lot and began to drive. Often, that summer, we'd take aimless detours. Sometimes we'd make wide loops around the city, sometimes we'd end up in a different county, sometimes we'd just get food. We got off I-80 close to home, and then I veered right, up into a neighborhood that I called the Heights, but its real name was something flatter. It just had hills that the rest of town didn't. One was steep enough that if you drove up it, there was a second where you couldn't see the road.

We curled up slowly through the Heights. The streets were

dark and the houses glowed yellow. The anger had leaked out of our silence. When I felt lost I'd flick my high beams on for brief bursts, but they never really let me see farther. They only made the things in front of me brighter, starker—a crooked mailbox, a fallen branch. As we rode in silence, the beams caught a glint so I braked. It was a doe, staring at us from the front yard of a red split-level. We saw her stomach pressed tight against her rain-clumped fur and murmured at the same time *Pregnant.* She stood still and watched us drive away.

Suburban deer always feel like a glitch, but I still saw them everywhere in Iowa City: eating leaves in the cemetery, congregating in the auditorium parking lot, walking through baseball fields. I always assumed they were lost and that their real home lay in the deep woods. But I learned that deer actually love the suburbs. They flock and multiply there for the same reason humans do: there are few predators, abundant resources, scattered patches of green to amble through.

In the living room of the house we rented, there were five brown doors but only one led to the street. Those Iowa homes were strange, cobbled together awkwardly from generations of tenants and owners, split and joined and re-split to accommodate new kinds of living. It was like existing alongside clumsy ghosts. It was like the Sims, where I built rooms without windows, forgot to put in hallways, added staircases to nowhere, ladderless pools. Now I know that even fake humans have needs—corridors, exits, light.

Back in the Heights we kept driving, making turns, backtracking when we hit dead ends. Rounding the corner, we saw her again. She must have been running straight through backyards as we were looping slowly around them. She didn't pause to look at us this time, she just streaked back into the dark.

We misunderstood each other often, but never in the car. It made aimlessness feel propulsive. It made gazing out a window feel like watching a movie. It made a montage out of sipping large Diet Dr.Peppers in the parking lot of the abandoned Kmart, making figure eights around blackened piles of snow. We'd park under the orange lamps and lay out all our Taco Bell on the dash. We'd laugh watching three teenagers bolt from the Dairy Queen carrying a stolen ice cream cake. The car was where we liked music the most. In winter, it got warmer than our house could. In summer, we went there to cool off. We should have done it more. We spent so many hours in bed, seething quietly right next to each other, neither of us thinking to simply leave the bed and get some air.

We reversed our path back to the busy road. People were down there. Light was down there. Near home, I saw a man's shadow beside him on the concrete and thought it was a black dog he was walking.

Storm Lake, Part 3

NOBODY KNEW WHAT STATE SHE left it in, and nobody knew what state it was in now. We knew she took almost nothing with her. We knew she never wanted to go back. We knew she had been in a fight with the water company for months before she left, and that she refused to pay her bill, though we didn't know why. We didn't know how she managed without running water. We heard from an acquaintance that the lights occasionally flickered on and off. It might now be a meth lab. It might contain a family of squatters. It might be gutted, and left unlocked, an open secret. It might have a hole through which the world poured in. Or it might be untouched, the exact same but rotting. I heard from Dad that there might be used maxi pads in grocery bags, large bills magpied away in old shoes, a nest in the chimney. A bassinet that someone meant to pass down through the family. A gun in the attic, or a missing gun.

It was now several months since I'd called her in the hospital. My desire to see her house had turned pressing. I knew my grandma was messy, but I'd only ever seen her messes confined to a suitcase, or a bedside table, or a car. Never had I seen her inhabit a space fully, and because of this, the old house grew in my imagination. I would be done with grad school in a year, and I knew if I didn't see it now, while I was still in Iowa, nobody in my family ever would. The house had been a great family mystery for years. For the last decade that my grandma lived there, she was alone. Only she knew what it looked like, how she'd lived. My dad would have the best guess, but when we got to talking about the house, he didn't offer much about how she might've left it. We theorized instead about what had happened to it since. My mom posited that the flickering lights were teenagers. My dad believed it had been emptied by thieves and squatters. My brothers thought the meth lab theory most likely, imagining the place filthy and condemned. I didn't know what I thought. When I looked it up on Google Street View, the house was shrouded by trees. When I looked at it via satellite, I could see only squares of brown and green. It hadn't burned down. That was all anyone could say for sure.

On Sunday morning, I sent an email to my family announcing my plan. I would set out for Storm Lake the following Friday. On Monday afternoon, I sat in my windowless office in the English building, booked a room in a Super 8, and texted Kylie, *I did it*. On Tuesday night, I ordered a nineteen-piece lock-picking kit from Amazon, and on Thursday night, it arrived. After dinner, Kylie sat on the couch trying to finish her work for the following week, because she didn't expect to get much done during our trip. I sat down next to her, as if to relax, then sprang up suddenly. *What?* she asked. *My kit!* I said brightly, remembering. I took out the practice padlock, made transparent to demystify the mechanisms I'd be attempting to outsmart. Then, I took the little jagged picks out one by one and began to jiggle them in the hole. It was a surprisingly indelicate art.

So you're just gonna like, she squinted at me, incredulous, *break in?* When I pictured myself going in, I was wearing gloves and heavy boots. I was gingerly lifting up cups and papers with an inquisitive expression, recording them, studying them, like an archaeologist.

Yeah, I said. *It doesn't seem hard.*

And then what?

I didn't answer as I concentrated on the practice lock. A minute or two passed, and suddenly, it swung open.

Look! I said, feeling more capable than usual.

I locked it again and stuck the picks in, watching, through clear plastic, each pin lift with grace up to the shear line. I seemed to have it down. It was time to try on the real deal.

On my front porch, in front of my locked door, I practiced the break-in. With my left hand, I raked the pick in and out of the keyhole, while my right gripped a torsion tool and pushed as hard as possible in the direction of entry, listening for the right pins to unclick, fingers raw, forehead hot and beading, my phone lit up by a YouTube tutorial that told me my problem was too much force, but really, it was blindness. The clear padlock had made a false promise; it had led me to believe that I could master an inscrutable object. After thirty unsuccessful minutes, Kylie beckoned me back inside.

Baby, I told you, she said, *it's not that easy.*

In the days leading up to my Storm Lake trip, both my dad and my grandma emailed me constantly. If I responded too

slowly, he sent emails with the subject *Earth to Emily*. She kept
adding to the list of valuables she'd like me to save, forgetting
for a moment how desperately she didn't want me to go in.
The items became etched in my brain. The solid mahogany
Henredon furniture. A bag of silver. A set of china she hoped
nobody had stolen. She seemed panicked, more so than usual.

   I asked:

*Do you have a utility bill or anything like that? a locksmith
would be able to make me a key, which I could then give to
you, but a document would help verify things*

She responded:

EMILY, I DON'T WANT THE DUMB THING OPENED UP.

   But the more my grandma told me not to go in, the more I
itched to do it. I was in high school when hoarding burst onto
the pop-psych scene, joining obesity and body dysmorphia as
one of many new afflictions caused by American excess. These
people—the messy, the fat, the appearance-obsessed—had, of
course, existed forever, but the world had begun to recognize
their afflictions as, at least on some level, a product less of choice
than of social and biochemical circumstance. Now, in addition
to quiet pity and the wrath of God, they got television shows.
Formerly milquetoast cable networks like TLC and A&E rein-
vented themselves as modern freak shows, purveyors of consumption taken to extremes. We got *My 600-lb Life, 19 Kids
and Counting, My Strange Addiction*, and a cottage industry ded-

icated just to hoarding shows. There was the original, *Hoarders*, plus *The Hoarder Next Door, Extreme Clutter, Confessions: Animal Hoarding,* and *Hoarding: Buried Alive.* Hoarding was added to the *DSM-5* in 2013 as a distinct disorder, where before it had just been a bullet point under the larger umbrella of OCD. It's diagnosed as the compulsion to acquire more and more things, combined with a fear of getting rid of them; an unhealthy attachment to material objects. The intensity of the attachment is crucial to a diagnosis, and though the *DSM* doesn't specify the material objects, unofficially, everybody knows that to be a proper hoarder, you have to be in love with junk. The shows teach us that the hoarder looks upon his mountains of empty Mountain Dew liters, newspapers, cat food tins, and decrepit garage-sale trinkets, and sees not trash but a kingdom.

My dad said my grandma was like this, but I'd never seen it for myself. I'd only ever seen hoarder houses on TV. I wanted to know how it felt to live in a trash kingdom. In emails, I peppered him with questions. *At first,* he said, *it was just the purple room.* The purple room was an empty bedroom. It began as a storage space for the usual detritus of family life, things brought out for occasions and then returned to their hiding places— boxes of Christmas decor, the fancy set of dishes. *Gradually,* he continued, *it spread to other rooms too.* The basement came next. His dad and his grandmother did their best to tend the pile, quartering it in these unseen rooms. Until it spread to the family room. I kept trying to get him to quantify the messiness. *Was it messy like you,* I asked, *or like TV?* He demurred, I pressed for details. *What kind of stuff was it? Clothes? Magazines? Trinkets?* He didn't say. *Did it bother you?* No, and on this he was firm. *Resilient* was the only adjective he used. *What did people think when they came over?* They didn't come over, he told me, they weren't allowed, and here, he did elaborate. He described grade school sleepovers on the cold cement floor of the garage, because his bedroom was upstairs, and upstairs was off-limits to visitors. By the time my mom visited Storm Lake, in the early '80s, the whole house was off-limits. She stayed instead at his grandparents' house, his grandparents who were neat and whom he loved most. Their house was full of warm food and quilts, photos and scrapbooks and baby blankets folded neatly in armoires, a TV set in a cabinet and a shag rug he could sit on right in front, watching cartoons as he ate a warm dinner.

─────

The definition of hoarding as compulsive garbage collecting is a relatively recent one. By this modern standard, my dad has never been a hoarder. You'd never see him on TV, because to parse his mess would be as impersonal as taking inventory in a warehouse. But he is a hoarder in the ancient sense, a Midas of plastic and cords, because what my dad did, does, will always do, is shop. He shopped when he was a kid with money earned from his newspaper route, in college, when he had no money and fell into a pit of credit card debt that decimated his finances for years. By the time I was born, he had enough money that he could finally accumulate without ruin.

In these early years, he worked constantly, returning from his law firm late at night only to resume work in his home office, crawl into bed for a few hours, and drive back to the city in the morning. Weekends were the only time he could shop. He left each store with a long, curling receipt and a cart filled with bags, sometimes two carts, sometimes three. When I was a baby, he'd take my brothers to Toys"R"Us. At the end, he always asked them the same question: *Would you rather be able to buy toys like this, or have Dad spend more time at home?* Their answer, every time, was toys.

As time wore on, he began to find office life increasingly intolerable—the suits, the pleasantries, the hierarchies of power that asked you to both give and receive obsequity. He loved the task of litigation, how it turned persuasion into a sport, and of course, he loved the money, its cushion and its froth, how it calmed him as it glinted. The rest was a distraction. So he began to work from home, a policy violation his firm quietly permitted because he made them so much money that they couldn't afford to lose him. In turn, they paid him less—still a lot, but less—and to my surprise, he accepted this trade. I'd never known him to accept less, nor would I call him a family man. But he wanted to be around. Home had his stuff and the people he knew best. What home didn't grant him was time. On the contrary, he began to work even more. He became tenser than ever. He developed a patch on his eyebrow where no hair would grow because he rubbed it so much with a worried thumb.

Then, right there in his home, he discovered an infinite mall. A bookseller had only just begun to dip its toe into the world of everything. Dad and Amazon scaled up side by side. Each year he worked harder at his job, each year he made more money, and each year Amazon made it easier for him to spend it. When Amazon began to allow third-party sellers, his world of digital commerce expanded in turn. When Amazon began algorithmically recommending products based on other users' spending habits, he acquiesced. Their habits became his. When Amazon provided free shipping on orders over ninety-nine dollars, he made sure to exceed that threshold every time.

One day in eighth grade, as we all watched *NCIS* in the living room, he announced to us that Amazon now offered free unlimited two-day shipping. *I just ordered a pack of AAA batteries*, he said, awed, *and it'll be here in two days*. Before, his buying had been limited by the material realities of in-store shopping. Weekends had only so many hours, and stores were open for only some of them. Amazon allowed him to shop at any hour, from any place, in quantities that far outstripped the capacity of a cart, a car, a basket, his arms. All he needed was a credit card and his thumb. Each day the porch filled with packages, dozens of them. He unwrapped the packages one by one and left the items on the kitchen counter, or the dining room table, in the corner of the entryway, at the bottom of the stairs. If he ran out of storage, he could buy more storage. If he ran out of house, he could buy more house. Amazon once called and asked, when my mom picked up, *Is this Mester*, not *The Mesters*, just *Mester*. When she said yes, they asked to speak to the head of purchasing, because they didn't think *Mester* could possibly be the name of a single, mortal man who had thirty pairs of the same wireless earbuds, fifty Leatherman multi-tools, a hundred USB cords.

I am exactly like him. I regard him the way a medical student regards a cadaver, awed and queasy because she's looking at a version of herself. Our accumulating feels biomedical, a heritable condition that switches on in some, lies dormant in others. The rest of my family isn't like my dad and me. My brothers make more money than I do but they buy far less. My mom's entire wardrobe occupies less than a quarter of the giant closet she shares with him. She is so unenthused by the prospect of owning more things that her rare shopping trips—to make her annual Ann Taylor Loft pilgrimage, to replace her favorite pair of shoes, to buy Christmas gifts—are undertaken not as recreational activities but dutiful errands.

I can't fathom her aversion. People hear dewy idealism in John Lennon's "Imagine," but all I've ever heard was a cruel paradox: imagine no possessions. As a child, I took his challenge seriously. I sat in my room and began to touch everything in it, taking stock. Was my cat a possession? The walls? My hands? A stoned friend once said to me *If the universe is constantly expanding, what is it expanding into?* Imagining a possessionless world felt like that.

I've loved shopping as long as I've grasped the concept of ownership. My parents watched my pupils dilate and skitter over the shelves the moment we entered a store. Wanting was the shape my world took, all my wonder and terror. Every Christmas, I effortlessly crafted a long, florid list of my desires while my brothers struggled to think of more than a couple things. I wanted a sister and a cat, a Barbie Jeep and the deluxe hundred-pack of colored pencils, world peace, a doll that could ingest food and regurgitate it into her backpack, a doll that could piss itself, a doll called Baby Tumbles whose only trick was a somersault, achieved by having a head many times heavier than her body. When boarding school kicked me out, I began buying things with my parents' credit card, the one I was supposed to use only for food and essentials. I lay in my bed in the Chicago suburbs, covered in apocrine sweat and pretzel dust, and ordered things my dormmates wore, cashmere sweaters and fifty-dollar gardenia body wash from France. By the time my parents noticed, two months later, I'd spent a thousand dollars. They read out the list of charges as I hung my head low, their faces showing bafflement, irritation, the same reaction they had when I put a box of Lucky Charms back in the pantry having picked out each marshmallow with my sticky little hands. But inside my shame, an air pocket opened: the amount I'd added to their bill was immaterial enough that it could almost have slipped past unnoticed. The sum that to me felt unfathomable was to them like the marshmallows. It was wrong to take the money, in theory, but the money, in practice, didn't matter, not to them. It was a spiritually dangerous thing for me to learn.

The credit card was rescinded. I wasn't trusted with one again until after college, when I returned to South Carolina and was given a card to use when babysitting my sister or filling their car with gas. When I began graduate school, I suddenly had a whole apartment to decorate, a brand-new teaching job to attire myself for, and most important, a refreshed sense of uncertainty about my life and what it might come to mean. My desire to outspend that uncertainty bumped up against the meager fact of my salary. But I soon found a loophole: the card. They'd forgotten to take it back, and I quickly learned it could be used on Amazon without detection, my handful of charges on the card statement indistinguishable from my dad's hundreds, like drizzle in the ocean. Sitting in my car in the parking lot of the English building, I ordered macramé wall hangings, ceramic knickknack jars, solar-powered stick-on lights to illuminate the creaky, darkened porch. It filled with packages, just like his did, and I tore them open in a shiny-eyed fugue, just like he did.

My dad and I shared a similarly unflappable belief that our excess was different from our predecessors'. He was not a hoarder like his mother because he had no use for useless objects. He didn't save yogurt containers or especially nice jam jars. He had no interest in tchotchkes, didn't care about getting things for free or at a discount, didn't scavenge odd furniture from the side of the road, accept brochures or free pens. He had no interest in nostalgia, did not maintain photo albums or hang on to birthday cards. He didn't even decorate, never rated the vague value of beauty. The only decorating I'd ever seen him do was on the walls of his office, where he hung a few items that plainly represented his interests: a magazine cover featuring Larry Bird, a photo of his favorite NFL coach, a tin sign of the oil company that supplied petroleum to his dad. There was no weird doll collection, no mountain of junk threatening to avalanche, just heaps of ordinary products, sealed in blister packaging. If he held a garage sale, it would just be a store.

The key difference between his hoarding and mine, I believed, was my penchant for returns: my constant buying was offset by my constant returning, which curled the unidirectional deluge of incoming products into a perpetual churning loop of deliver and return, deliver and return. I kept only what I wanted, and the rest was flung as far away from me as possible. As packages came in, I tore them open and decided their fate.

Only a few items produced an immediate sense of joy. They went swiftly to their new homes in cabinets and drawers, clicking into my life like Lego blocks. Rarely did an item receive an immediate no. The vast majority produced ambivalence, and these—a pair of pants that I could stand but not sit in, a candle so exquisite that I'd probably never light it—were stacked into a purgatorial corner of my room. Every day I passed by the stack and every day it grew, a heap of decisions I deferred until its size became unignorable. Unignoring it took hours. First, I held each item aloft. But holding wasn't enough. I had to try on every piece of clothing, sniff every scent, consider all possible futures, all possible selves, until I could determine that none of them required the object I now gripped in my hands. This step was full of fits and starts, feverish activity followed by catatonic pauses that found me clammy and dazed cross-legged on the floor, or motionless in my bed staring at my phone. Sometimes I gave up and fell asleep. Finally, often after being pressed gently by Kylie, I'd print out shipping labels, seal the boxes with Wirecutter-recommended extra-sticky packing tape, fill my car, and then drive around to UPS and USPS and FedEx to drop them all off. When post offices filled after Christmas like gyms in January, I cast glances at the amateur returners who brought piles of loose items, no boxes, no tape, just barcodes on their phone that they fumbled for as a line snaked out the door. I was an expert. I was so good at returns that workers would sometimes compliment my packing, how I covered the new label with tape, blacked out the old one with Sharpie, secured the weak flaps, sorted boxes by carrier. I knew which UPS stores charged you a dollar to mail a USPS package, the maximum dimensions of a FedEx drop box, the fact that some carriers didn't let you use bags, only boxes. When I returned home I gathered up all the paper scraps from the printed shipping labels, then neatly flattened and stacked boxes from the items I'd kept—too many of them. I ferried the unrecyclable materials—tape, foam peanuts, plastic pillows, wrap—into a trash bag. As I walked back from the curb, bagless and boxless, I felt an extraordinary relief of elimination, like the best shit you've ever taken in your life, the kind that leaves you feeling almost holy, floating upward. My corner would be empty, and in a few weeks, my money would be deposited back into my bank account as if I'd been paid for labor. I'd rid myself of excess. Nothing had been wasted.

———

The night before our trip to Storm Lake, after I failed to pick my own lock, I came in from the porch and sat down in the living room. As a sort of preparation, Kylie was in our room watching an old episode of *Hoarders*. I'd never actually watched the show, and I didn't want to now. The type of decrepit voyeurism I preferred was ruins. I sat on the couch and opened my laptop. While Kylie watched ranch homes overtaken by boxes, I marveled at abandoned subway stations underneath City Hall in Manhattan, leviathan roller coasters swallowed by shrubs, chaises in the natatorium of a crumbling Catskills resort, old factories where they used to make sugar or toy trains, the ghostly former headquarters of Bulgaria's Communist Party, an Olympic pool in Berlin now filled with brown water, a palace in Namibia now filled with sand. It was thrilling to gaze at the

visible passage of time. Even spaces that would've been unremarkable in the intact past felt profound in the rotted present.
When I read *Huckleberry Finn* in middle school, I was fascinated
by the scene where Huck and Jim discover an abandoned house
floating down the Mississippi. The pair find a dead man and Jim
tells Huck to look away, something about ghosts and leaving
the past be. They turn away from the dead man, who is later
revealed to be Huck's own father, but in my memory this detail
was a footnote, overshadowed by what happens next: they reap
the spoils. They find an old straw hat, dirty calico dresses, a bottle with milk in it and a rag stopper for the baby to suck, but no
woman, no baby. They take with them some knives and combs.

Ruins are easy to find. On the fringes of American towns
sit dormant warehouses and theaters and sanatoriums, per-
meated by flora and fauna, reduced mostly to dust and rebar.
Teenagers go and drink there, urban explorers come armed
with headlamps and GoPros. Whoever abandoned these places
doesn't seem to lose sleep over their fate. At most there is a
little padlock or chain, maybe a sign that says KEEP OUT, a limp
gesture but nothing more.

It's harder to find an abandoned place that isn't ruined but
full and frozen in time. A floating house, where somebody left
their whole life behind. As I practiced picking the lock to my
grandma's house, I pictured the door coughing up a cloud of
dust as it creaked open, like in mummy movies when they
crowbar open a tomb. I wanted to know what it felt like to
breathe fifteen-year-old air. I wanted to read newspapers from
before I was born. I wanted to find the bag of silver and my
dad's stuffed animals and the clothes still waiting in the hamper.

I wanted to unstick the past from its amber. I wanted to read her mail. There was also, at that very moment, a home that she currently lived in, a home I could probably, if I pressed, convince her to let me into, no lock picking necessary. But I'd never asked. To parse an abandoned life was exploration, it was genealogy, it was archaeology, it was ghosts. That I could knock on her door and find her life as she lived it, that was the cadaver. I averted my eyes.

In the other room, as Kylie watched *Hoarders*, she kept murmuring *Oh god, oh god*, in awe. I glanced over at the screen. A man in his thirties with long red hair was standing in a kitchen among towers of pizza boxes and cans of Coke Zero. *How can they see that and not care?* she asked later, as a mother of two weaved through a living room of boxes. *How can they be that obsessed with trash?* she continued. *Watching this makes me want to clean.*

I was not like Kylie. Where she was active, I was sluggish. Where she was direct, I wrung my hands. Where she was clean, I was disordered. In boarding school, the dorm advisors did room checks once a week, and I always failed. Each week, the failures compounded. The clutter turned to mess, the mess turned to a pile, stagnant and mudbound. Whenever it reached this point, the school threatened dire consequences, and so I'd clean the room in a three-hour fervor and then lie down in my bed panting, elated with purification.

When I met Kylie at the beginning of grad school, I had lived in my apartment for several months, but there were still boxes in my living room that I hadn't unpacked, a half-finished bookshelf sitting in the closet, vegetables rotting in the crisper, and a bedside table filled with empty plates and cups. I functioned a bit better than I had in high school, but a version of this was how I'd always lived. Kylie was diligent, functional in a way I didn't understand. She woke up on Sunday mornings to clean the whole house while I remained unconscious until noon. Mess bothered her, and I suppose it bothered me too, but it catalyzed only one of us. If she looked at my ear and spotted a bit of wax, she'd stick her finger in to get it. If she owned something, it was because she either loved it or needed it. She took a shower every single day and didn't view it as a chore. To me, this was incredible.

———

Before we headed out on Friday morning, I packed some sweatpants, an old paint-stained T-shirt, a flashlight, sturdy shoes, a button-up shirt if I wanted to introduce myself to neighbors, a jacket for the predicted rain, my laptop, a tray of giant Costco muffins for the drive. I kicked myself for not remembering thick rubber gloves, but I figured I could just get those at Walmart. I considered a ventilation mask. I double-checked to make sure we'd brought the lock-picking kit.

My dad had warned me that the drive would be terrible, but there were barely any cars on the road. The divided highway narrowed into a two-lane, which generated a bracing slap of air whenever another car passed us fast in the opposite direction and we briefly, sharply, crossed winds. We passed Hubbard and Jewell and Coalville and Manson, Early and Newell and Sac City and Nemaha, which greeted us with a sign bearing its population, eighty-five, and a slogan:

A "MIGHTY" SMALL TOWN. Storm Lake's sign sat beneath a giant replica of the town's lighthouse, and I remembered that it was named for an actual lake, which abutted it, big enough to drive a speedboat through.

We headed straight to her house. We passed the lakeside hotel and its attached water park, the eyeglass store on the town's main drag that used to be Len's gas station, the Dollar General and the Dollar Tree, my grandma's preferred dollar franchise, because everything is actually a dollar. We saw a little brick structure, no bigger than a bathroom, with a drive-up teller window. We passed the meatpacking plant, a collection of tall white blocks that now bore the red-and-yellow logo of Tyson Foods, which had acquired IBP for $3 billion in 2001. Most of the other changes Storm Lake had undergone were invisible from the car, but you could see glimpses of them. There was a Hy-Vee and a Fareway, but also Valentina's Meat Market and an African grocery store. When I visited my grandma as a kid, we ate at a place called G Witters, which I kept getting confused with G. Williquors, a different restaurant down the street, but G. Williquors was now called BozWellz and G Witters was now a pho restaurant that sat beside a dance club called El Mariachi.

Grandma had been emailing me all week. My impending trip had kicked up her memory. Storm Lake contained VERY PAROCHIAL LUTHERANS. It contained THE NEIGHBOR I AM AMBIVALENT ABOUT. She mentioned that the hospital, which sat right behind the house, might want to buy the land from her. I HAVE ABSOLUTELY NO SENTIMENTS FOR THE PLACE, she said, BUT EMPTYING IT IS PROBLEMATIC.

The GPS announced my grandma's street, and then our destination. I pulled into the driveway, next to a blocky white van and a trailer that clearly wasn't hers. I wondered in which year—the fifth, the ninth, the twelfth?—the neighbors decided enough time had passed, and that they could probably park there. We got out of the car and stood still on the lawn for a minute, facing the house. It was a small ranch with tan brick, beige siding, a white-doored garage, a front stoop shaded by trees. I was struck by how unabandoned it looked. The front curtains were all drawn, but they would've been like that when she lived there, too. Someone had kept cutting the grass. Only the front hedges seemed off, but I couldn't figure out why. Kylie noticed me squinting at them. *They're supposed to be below the window*, she reminded me—these covered the glass entirely.

We walked up the front stoop, and at my feet I saw a stack of soggy newspapers. Excitedly, I shook one out of its plastic bag. *Oh my god*, I raised my eyebrows like a gossip. *I bet the date on this is gonna be crazy.* My face fell a bit when I unrolled the wet paper. It was only a couple years old. That was when Kylie noticed the basement window, which had been obscured by the shadow of a towering pine. A browning bed sheet had been hung to cover it, but the sheet had fallen, revealing a view of the inside. We knelt and peered in at a sea of cardboard boxes, not neatly stacked, but heaped. We dutifully murmured the labels on the boxes. *Campbell's, Wheaties, Chex, Bounce, Ore-Ida.* We saw a wooden kitchen chair, and on it, a little row of the travel-size toiletries she loved to collect from hotels. We saw, in the dirt we were squatting on, a small rodent skull, a few clumps of fur still in the cavities, teeth still perfectly intact.

Isn't it funny that teeth are considered bone, I mused to Kylie. She said gently, *They're not.*

We went around to the backyard. There were the patio stones my dad had laid, with a set of steps leading down to the basement door. But the steps had collapsed, the stones scattered like blocks, as if a giant put his foot down. Someone, maybe a neighbor, had strung orange construction fencing across the yard's perimeter, as if to say *keep out*, or maybe *this place isn't safe*, or more likely, *this isn't mine*.

We walked to the next window, which was mostly covered by a curtain, but there was a slice of window at the bottom where the curtain didn't reach. We could see just a foot or two of floor in front of us, covered in a blanket of paper and plastic that pressed up against the window. My eyes darted from word to word. Powder eyeshadow samples from Avon with a card that said GET GORGEOUS: FALL FORECAST 1998, an unused box of Kleenex, unopened notepads, fake plants, several empty cream cheese containers, brown and cracked, a piece of paper that said PEGGY in a child's handwriting, and beneath it PLEASE DO NOT FOLD OR BEND. There was a box of expanding wallets, thirteen-inch capacity, a corded phone half pulled out of the wall, Coke bottles (not Diet, she hated Diet) scattered on the floor, a Folgers tin, a fan of checks and bills wedged behind the light switch, and a wooden spice rack on the wall that, through the smudged glass, I briefly mistook to be filled with doll heads. I saw a box containing unscented baby wipes and another that said MAGIC CHEF. There was a letter on the floor that read *Dear Client, We have scheduled the following appointment for you with* WILBUR BOGGS *to obtain information for*—but the rest was covered by more trash. There was an Ensure coupon, a can of Natural Light, which I didn't know she drank, a box of prunes, which I didn't know she ate, a copy of the *Financial Times* from 1996, a few Chinese takeout boxes smeared with brown sauce, and at the bottom, a dead wasp. I couldn't see the top of the dining room table, but I noticed it still had its hang-tag: HENREDON. Beyond this patch, we couldn't see much; the rest of the house was too dark and far from the window. But I could say this with certainty, and did, aloud, to Kylie. *Nobody has been inside this house.*

No break-in. No meth lab. No marauders. No squatters. No thieves. It was her mess, undisturbed, not gone and not even rotting. This was what I'd said I wanted, but now, my breath fogging up the window, my body separated from the abandoned room by only this pane of glass, I felt something I hadn't expected: fear. The places I found online were eerie, yes, but they only contained traces of their pasts. You might see a plate or a letter or a broken chair, but for the most part, these places felt well and properly *abandoned*. They were emptied of life long ago. Walls and windows had broken and light shone through them, making room for airy, elegant words like *beautiful* or *fascinating*. Moss and grass grew. These ruins moved with time, were crumbled by it. The one in front of me was sealed and airless. I thought her house might feel like a time capsule, but it felt like she'd never left at all.

We could try the garage door, I offered quietly. We walked over to it, lifted it a few inches, and surprisingly, it complied. As we kept lifting, the heap that had been pressed up against it began sliding through the gap. Empty bottles of Nesquik and Tahiti

Treat Fruit Punch. A can of Cherry Coke with a design I recognized from the '90s. Children's activity books from before I was born. The door was now open about eight inches. We both looked at each other, realizing, then, that the whole thing would lift if we wanted it to. We could get in this way.

But we didn't want to lift it any further. Instead, in silence, we closed it again.

By now, it was early evening. Not one but two pupusa restaurants sat down the street from our hotel. You couldn't buy a pupusa anywhere near Iowa City. We chose one called El American. It was a small place, just a couple booths and a window. As we waited for our food, we looked around at the walls. Edward Hopper's *Nighthawks* hung above two portraits of Marilyn Monroe. There was a plaque commemorating Michael Jordan, a sculpture of two geese taking flight. On our table, there was an open copy of *La Voz*, a Spanish-language newspaper that served three surrounding towns. On the cover, the words *DACA* and *Trump*. The congressional quadrant of the state that included Storm Lake was overwhelmingly white and Republican. This was the district of Steve King, a congressman so racist that his own party would eventually kick him out.

When we checked into the Super 8, it was nine o'clock at night. As Kylie finished writing a paper, I answered the flurry of emails my dad had sent asking if I'd arrived, what I'd seen, if I'd gone in. I sent pictures—the shrub over the door, the crumbled back porch, the view through the windows. I'd found the mess unsettling. My dad seemed underwhelmed. He'd seen the mess. He'd lived in it. When he'd predicted a ruin, he may also have been hoping for one.

The phone pinged with an email from my grandma. She wanted me to call her. As I dialed, I sat on the slippery floral bedspread gnawing on the lock pick. She picked up immediately and started speaking in a frenzy. Her life came spilling out of her. *I never wanted to marry him,* she began. *Used to brag his parents were so unemotional but they were just strange. On my wedding night I thought oh my god what have I . . .* She trailed off. *I hated being home, used to dream of leaving even when he was little. I can't figure out how I got along with everyone else's kids but not mine.* There was no room to interject, but I needed to make some kind of vocal gesture to let her know I was still there, still listening. I didn't want to *mhm,* which seemed to signal condescending agreement, or *ah,* which would signal detached comprehension, so I just murmured *ohh,* kept saying it, my soft *ohh ohh*s floating beneath her words, which came out of her in a fast and forceful way that sounded at times like anger, at other times like pleading. *Have you ever tried to live with someone for years that you can't stand,* she asked, and at this point, it was hard to tell who she was referring to, her husband or my dad. *I used to just dream of leaving . . . wouldn't walk across the sidewalk to see . . . Bullshit. I don't need or want him . . . I had a nice house and didn't take care of it . . . death would be a lot easier . . .* and then, this refrain, her voice as small and quivering as I'd ever heard it:

I wrecked my life. I wrecked my life. Oh god.

You didn't . . . I offered, my voice cracking from disuse. I didn't know what else to say.

Kylie went to bed around midnight. I knew already that I'd be up until morning. As she slept next to me, I opened my laptop and decided, finally, to watch *Hoarders.* A lot of their messes looked like the one I'd just seen, though many were even worse. But while Kylie had marveled at the hoarders' psychology, I was startled now by the disconnect between mess and maker. Where the homes were extreme, the hoarders themselves were often not. In a group that was supposed to be driven by obsession and compulsion, I was struck by how often the hoarders *didn't* seem abnormally attached to their messes. By how many of them *didn't* seem especially driven to collect things. By how many *did* see the mess for what it was and were just as bothered by it as the viewer. The man with the pizza boxes didn't seem to keep them because he loved them. The mother of two shook and wept at her kingdom.

The TV show wanted me to see people obsessed and compelled, but far more than that, I saw people who, somewhere along the normal cycle of consumption, had been paralyzed into a deep ambivalence. Our living naturally creates piles of disorder, and it requires tremendous effort to work against that entropy. Sometimes it still amazes me how quickly the laundry basket fills, how easily milk spoils, how if I forget to take the bags out for trash day one week, their amount will have doubled by next time. The hoarders' messes might've been extreme, but they were rooted in a painfully familiar inertia. *I think it's difficult to do . . . anything*, said the woman with eight hundred shoes, out of whose home they hauled three tons of garbage. *And being a hoarder*, she added haltingly, *it's more difficult for me.* When I played the Sims as a kid, I discovered you could set your Sims' free will to "off," which meant they no longer automatically did things like eat, sleep, and go to the bathroom; you had to tell the Sim to do it. At first, it was fun, dictating how often a fake human could pee. But it quickly became tedious when I realized how much of living is dedicated to these mundane tasks, and how, if you are not programmed to do them almost without thinking, they consume you, and you again become a child. You want to make friends with the neighbors, try on outfits, and become a movie star. But before you know it, your kitchen swarms with flies as you rock back and forth in a puddle of urine.

In one episode, the girlfriend of a hoarder stood in front of a dumpster and held aloft a broken lamp. The shade was all bent, the base grimy. *You don't want this*, she asked him, *do you?* To look at a thing and know what to do with it requires a series of decisions and actions that a healthy person can make with ease. In the girlfriend's mind, I could see that the decisions were easy, almost instantaneous. *It doesn't work, and I can't fix it. And so I won't keep it. It has no use.* But her boyfriend, who owned the lamp, looked pained. He couldn't bring himself to say what he did or didn't need. He didn't necessarily look at the lamp and see treasure, just like he didn't look at his piles of trash and see no problem. He saw an insurmountable task from which he quietly turned away. His so-called attachment to objects seemed, more than anything, to be a problem of ontology. He couldn't find the line between value and valuelessness, between want and need, between satiety and hunger, between thing and thing. To lift one object from the pile was to hoist the whole mess, every decision tugging a thousand more behind it.

I was never meant to be a mother. I heard my grandma say it my whole life—*I didn't want kids* or *I enjoyed teaching children but not raising one* or *He was a problem from the start.* She said these things to my dad even when he was a kid, right in front of him, regretting his childhood before he'd even finished it. For a long time, I was incredulous—it didn't seem like my grandma— but I understood now. Whether or not she'd wrecked her life, whether or not motherhood was the thing that wrecked it, she'd ended up on the wrong side of her ambivalence. Mother-hood was the choice that made all the others—the house, the husband, the town, the job—irreversible. She'd never been able to separate one regret from another.

The American Dream, as we know it, is abundance. It's a dream to amass houses, children, cars. It's a dream to collect things of value. But it is an equally American dream to be able to abandon, drop everything, to jettison, without guilt, any-thing that weighs you down. The first time my family moved, we hurried off to the new house and left our small brick bun-galow a mess, but because my parents couldn't afford not to sell it, we had to go back and haul everything out. All summer, on the front lawn, we sorted the house into dusty piles: keep, give away, trash. There was so much to sort through. Some of the keeps went to the new house, and many of them went to cav-ernous storage spaces in the outer suburbs. The next time we moved, we did the same thing. The piles in the storage spaces grew. The piles in the new house grew. The third and biggest house filled up like the rest. In college, they bought another, this time in South Carolina. They went to stay there for the summer, and when August came, they decided that actually, they didn't want to return. They hurriedly enrolled my sister in a new school. They bought replacements for all the things they'd left in Illinois. This time, they didn't have to sell the old house, didn't have to pack it up, and so it sat there collecting dust, food still in the fridge, lights still on in the rooms. It is an unimaginable privilege to do this. The practical difficulties of extracting yourself from responsibility—a home, a job, a marriage—are so daunting that many people never do it at all. Leaving requires resources that most people do not have. There are debts to settle, boxes to pack, replacements to find. And what comes after leaving is daunting, too; you're left to carry your entire life on your back. But abandoning? That's much simpler. You see an insurmountable task from which you turn away. You see a new life. Then, you run.

———

In the months leading up to my Storm Lake visit, I began to understand the limits of abandonment. The measures I took to undo my own consumption were beginning to fail. There were no clean breaks anymore. I winced as I threw away rotted produce, stuffed flattened Amazon boxes into blue bins, hauled bags of sweaters to the Salvation Army. Half of what I virtuously recycled would probably become garbage anyway, and so too would my compost. The clothing I hauled to the donation bins would end up not in the closet of a grateful mom of three or a young woman in need of a job-interview suit, but in by-the-pound liquidation sales, as industrial rags and sofa stuffing, or across the globe, where the scraps were sold for pennies on the dollar. At best. Often, those countries didn't want our scraps either, and it is they who finally must declare the stuff garbage. Before, getting rid of stuff brought me relief. But now in my brain a pile had formed where each discarded item lived. I could throw it halfway around the world, but it would always be mine. All my belongings—past, present, and future—were a big belly I dragged across the floor. I began to doubt the sturdiness of my floors, the capacity of my bedroom, the tenacity of the ceilings. It felt like everything would come crashing down. I began to move gingerly, slowly, as if apologizing to the ground.

But I didn't stop buying. Kylie became more and more frustrated with the boxes that piled up outside our door. Our household needs were met, but each day I invented a new one. Rather than dissuade the buying, my environmental guilt lent it a new shape. We needed to switch from liquid to bar soap, we needed a self-draining soap dish, we needed to buy glass containers for our body wash and detergent, we needed a receptacle to store our plastic grocery bags, then we needed reusable canvas bags, alternatives to plastic wrap, alternatives to paper towels, alternatives to everything. A single twelve-dollar bottle of body wash wrapped in plastic and cardboard traveled thousands of miles to my doorstep, on ships and planes, then on trucks and more trucks, only to be rejected because I realized I wanted to buy a refillable version, to be more eco-friendly. So the process began again, the damage not reversed but doubled, and at the end of it, the bottle wasn't resold, but thrown away too, because if I didn't want it, why would anyone else?

Before I understood the complexities of capitalism as a system, I learned how to use the word. I began to refer to capitalism the way people on the extreme ends of luck talk about God: as a mysterious force to which all bad or absurd things could be attributed. And because it was beyond my control, I decided that I wasn't responsible for my role within it. I could show up to elections and protests every so often, donate a little money, like my mom did on the one Catholic mass she went to each year. I could retweet petitions, stew unproductively in class guilt, but beyond that, capitalism, like God, was a force so large as to be inconceivable. This was the way my dad talked about the economy. The economy had a long arm but no hands, and the men who controlled it spoke of it like weather. Anytime I felt friction between what I did and what I believed, I muttered *No ethical consumption* again and again. This axiom was the perfect form of class consciousness: it made me feel wise to the injustice of the world, but also absolved me of using, or even acknowledging, whatever power I had to change it. Eating meat or not, shopping at Amazon or not, composting or not: What difference would it really make? I felt, when I consumed, that while my individual participation in the system would unavoidably augment its power, revoking my participation did nothing to diminish it. If consumption would always make me guilty, then perhaps it was more gratifying to guiltily consume, which at least produced charged, frothy sensations—shame, glee—than to abstain, which, like sexual abstinence, promised that I would feel neither sensation, and that somehow, maybe, in this void, a sense of weightless calm would spread.

———

Earlier that week, I'd promised my grandma I'd stop by the house that had belonged to my dad's grandparents. After they moved out in the '80s to go to a nursing home, it fell into my grandma's possession. Since then, she'd never touched it. The city kept sending her notices: the grass needed mowing, the garage needed painting. I'd seen long lawns and peeling paint all over town, so it seemed strange that the city should care so much about hers. She'd been fending them off for years.

IF YOU GO, WILL APPRECIATE YOUR ASSESSMENT,

BUT THINK IT IS A WASTE OF YOUR TIME,

JUST LIKE MY YEARS THERE WERE.

My dad's grandparents were tidy. At this house, there would be no mess. Maybe this house, I could stomach entering.

A few weeks earlier, Kylie had shown me her baby book, a type of memento I'd heard of but never actually seen. We sat on our bed and touched the bound cover that bore a photo of baby Kylie, a book about her life before she knew it. On each page, her mother had meticulously handwritten the small details of her baby's days. *Kylie was a bit fussy this afternoon. Kylie did so well at her doctor's appointment. Kylie especially loves her baby swing.* This type of record was miraculous to me. Kylie's family, unlike mine, was the type who valued their collective memory, who saw reason to preserve the kind of details that in the present can feel unremarkable. Kylie had kept journals as long as she'd been able to write. They sat in a large plastic tub in her closet. As a child, I would get pretty diaries at the bookstore only to write in them once and never see them again. Kylie also had dozens of childhood photos and videos, not just posed ones from special events, but ones of her playing on the carpet of her parents' first apartment, arranging stuffed animals on the back of her couch, eating spaghetti. My dad had so many cameras, an array of camcorders and film cameras and DSLRs and cheap point-and-shoots. I'd heard the rapid-fire shutter clicks of his cameras as they captured high-definition frame-by-frame photos of us crossing Abbey Road in London, us opening presents on Christmas, us playing soccer. But the footage had no home. New cameras were always rotating in as the old ones rotated to the attic, or to the storage spaces he maintained, or else to other houses he owned, and in those cameras were rolls of film, memory cards, cassette tapes, their contents never to be resurrected into the present because they'd never been pinned to a stable past. Nearly three decades ago, Kylie's parents put into boxes a blanket, a lock of hair, a onesie, grade school stories, even teeth, in the belief that someday she might want to take out the past and touch it. In the time since, so much had changed. She lost her dad a few years ago, suddenly. She'd drifted from her mom. And here was this baby book, like a thread between worlds. I wanted to create, for myself, this kind of artifact.

As we drove through town, it was hard to tell which houses were abandoned and which weren't. A lot had slumping porches. Some had open garages and kids playing in the yard. Some had long silver wheelchair ramps leading up to their front doors, contrasting sharply with the old wood.

I stopped in front of a small gray house. It was faded like an old picture, shrinking back from the curb and slumping in the shadow of the houses next door. It was even more abandoned than the rest. Before I saw the number, I knew this was it. We went around to the alley and parked on the grass.

The city was right: the garage needed repainting. So much paint had peeled that the only remaining bits hung off the wood in delicate little spindles, like dripping lace. We approached the garage and leaned our faces to the window. Through a broken pane I could see a rusted Mercedes-Benz with plates dated 1976, a pale yellow pickup truck that looked just as old, and in the truck bed, a cardboard box that said CATSUP—TWELVE BOTTLES.

We walked beside the clothesline, which led to the back of the house. *Uh oh*, Kylie said, pointing to a broken corner of the kitchen window. Had somebody broken in?

We moved to the window on the other side of the kitchen. It was set a little higher, so I stood on my toes and craned my neck to see through it. All I saw was a patch of bright white. At first, I thought it was reflecting the sky outside. But it wasn't a reflection. The ceiling wasn't there. I was staring up through the window at the sky itself. Where there should've been a peaked roof, there was a gaping hole. Someone had thrown a small ladder onto the roof, the kind you use to climb into a pool.

A falling tree must've caved in the kitchen roof, and through it birds had flown and nested. Who knew how many years since. Looking through another window, we saw the floor and the countertops and the sink, all covered with feathers and twigs and fluff. Every surface looked like a nest. There were a few old 7UP cans, the kind that came before pull tabs, lying next to a cabinet that had been left ajar. Someone besides the birds had been there too.

We moved along to the other windows. We didn't say much, just repeated, in low voices, *oh god*. The couches, the chairs, the table, the old radio, all of it crusted in a thick pale orange substance made up of bird shit and mouse shit and mold. The view into the bedroom was dim but I could see the edges of their nice sheets, their cream-colored quilt trimmed with tiny pom-poms, the brass bed perfectly made, and all of it infested. One window looked onto their dining table and chairs. A single drawer sat on the rug, having been pulled out, by someone, from the large chest beside it. The drawer was full of old letters and papers. Beside it was a stack of photo albums.

We walked up the steps to the front door, stepping over a pile of shattered glass that must've been the porch lamp. Through the picture window we could see into the living room. Its contents were spare, neatly arranged, and rotted. The letters from the city must've actually been condemnation notices, I was sure of it. It looked like a nightmare. I noticed, now, the shag carpet on the living room floor. I noticed that my eyes had begun to tear up. If I pressed my nose hard enough against the glass, I could see two little midcentury armchairs sitting in front of a wood-cabinet television set that looked no newer than 1965. It was this scene that I kept returning to later, that TV being silently watched by the chairs, in the hotel and in the restaurant and on the drive home. A teacher once asked me if I believed in ghosts, and I said, emphatically, no. *But I bet*, he said, *you wouldn't want to wear a suit owned by a dead man*. Standing in front of the house, I remembered that this type of haunting, too, has a name: *possessed*.

Not once did I remember my lock-picking kit. Not once did

I want to step inside. I stood there for a few more minutes squinting through the grimy window. Then, quietly, I turned away.

On the drive back to town, the lake and the fog blended together into an off-white screen. We parked at the Super 8 and walked to our room. It was freezing. I got under the blankets and sent all the pictures to my parents. *It's really bad*, I said. *Really bad.*

My dad responded immediately. He was angry at her. He'd opened so many Christmas gifts on that shag rug.

Christmas has always been his favorite holiday. As my siblings became adults, the gifting scaled up, not down. The presents weren't stacked, but heaped, spilling across the floor as if the tree were an overturned tractor trailer. The gift unwrapping began on Christmas Eve and my dad was always the one to start it. While the rest of us were at the table finishing dessert, he was thrumming with excitement. He'd want to open them all that night, and my mom had to gently remind him that if we opened them all now, there would be none on Christmas Day. He'd zip around gleefully, grabbing presents from the pile and handing them to us as we sat on couches and chairs. In minutes, we'd each be drowning in our own little gift pile, unable to see over it, pinned to our seats.

His gifts were utilitarianism at its luxurious peak—fancy wireless headphones, robotic vacuum cleaners, top-of-the-line phone chargers. Our gifts to him had to be the opposite. We had to buy him things he'd never think to want, objects with no use beyond beauty and nostalgia. Each year I'd struggle to think of a new little token. I found photos of his hometown on eBay, sports memorabilia, decorative glass globes to be placed on his desk. When you presented him with your gift, he'd place it politely on his chair, waiting until everyone else had opened theirs, at which point you'd urge him to open yours, excited to see if you'd finally cracked it, if you'd finally given him something that excited him as much as his Amazon boxes did when he opened them. But he'd just smile sheepishly, say thank you, and put the gift aside, where it would be swallowed into disuse.

Years after Storm Lake, after I'd left Iowa, I came across a famous Robert Hayden poem. My dad didn't seem to like poetry, ornate and meandering as it was. We rarely saw anything the same way, and this included each other. He thought I was soft, indolent, and ungrateful, I thought he was hardened, selfish, and unmerciful. We both agreed he'd gone to great effort to cushion me from scarcity. But I thought he'd been poisoned by the effort, and he thought I'd been ruined by the cushion.

The poem was generous in a way I hadn't been. It described him as I saw him, and also as he saw himself. It was about a father getting up early on a Sunday to chop wood for his family. He's tired from a week of hard work, but he has to keep them warm. No one thanks him, ambivalent as they are toward this man whose care is made less generous by the anger it leaves in its wake. *What did I know, what did I know,* the poem ends, *of love's austere and lonely offices?*

I framed it and gave it to him that Christmas. The poem called it love, and this was the closest I could get to saying it. Later, my mom told me that he'd hung the poem above his desk. It was the closest he could get too.

That night, in the Super 8, neither Kylie nor I could get to sleep.
We lay in bed for hours, talking about what we saw, and what
we should do next. *Why did all of that scare us?* we wondered.
Technically, we reasoned, her house wouldn't have been scary
if she were still living there. It would just be messy. And technically, the bird house was just what happens when the outside
world gets in. That led to more questions. We asked them out
loud, like children. *Is it scarier for a house to be empty or full? If the
bird house is what happens when the outside world gets in, then why
doesn't the outside world look as bad as the bird house? Do you think
you'd get sick if you breathed in that air? Do you think we should've
stood further from the window? Why am I scared of bird shit? Why am
I scared of that TV? Why am I scared of spiders but a dog isn't? Who
opened that drawer? Were they scared? Will the ceiling collapse? Will
the floor collapse? Did she really live like that?* And finally, *What are
we going to do with these houses?*

At two or so, she drifted off to sleep. At three or four, I
followed her. I don't remember my dreams, if I had them. I
slept heavy.

The next morning, we went to Hy-Vee to get flowers. I
stood in front of the buckets of stems googling *what flowers for
death?* "Sweet Child o' Mine" came on over the speakers as the
cashier-in-training rang me up. *I love this song*, I said to no one
in particular. Her supervisor gently led her through each step.
*Now we add some baby's breath. Now we want to wrap them so they
don't freeze.*

My dad wanted me to visit the cemetery. It was out in

the cornfields, where yesterday's fog still hadn't lifted. We followed a gravel road until we reached an iron gate and parked
on a patch of browned grass. Immediately, we both wished
we'd brought thicker coats. The weather was cold for October,
gloomy in a way that felt too obvious. Everywhere, cold gray
rain. My shoes, heavy Doc Martens that had kept my feet dry
through many winters, began to leak. I looked for the graves,
searching for my last name. I saw familiar ones from my grandma's stories: *Demers* and *Grell* and *Orland*. My eyes scanned
the tall slabs you imagine when you hear the word *tombstone*,
but then I realized that graves are expensive, and she wouldn't
have paid for something so steep. I started looking lower to the
ground, at the little engraved blocks that jutted slightly out of
the grass like cobble, something you could trip over but not
run into. Still nothing. My feet were now soaked with ground-
water. The wind was whipping at my wet hands. Kylie was
freezing, so I told her to go turn on the car and wait for me.
Frustrated, I kept walking until I saw a field of stones set into
the ground, flat, like sidewalk plaques. I knew these were the
cheapest. I knew they would be here, and they were.

The stones overlooked the cornfield, empty and brown
now because the growing season was over. A hundred little
sparrows fed from a puddle of freezing rain. There was a stone
for my dad's grandparents, and next to it, a stone for mine.
My grandfather's said 1931–1987. When Len died, he and my
grandma hadn't slept in the same bed for several years. The
money he'd lost had built silence between them. When he was
fifty-seven, when my dad was thirty, when my oldest brother
was about to turn one, Len had a heart attack while plowing

the driveway. The ambulance got lost on the way to him, even though it was only a five-minute drive. It was January. He lay on the frozen ground, his wiry body bundled in a coat. His head was bald and light brown like a peanut shell, his eyes open. By the time they lifted him into the warm ambulance, he was already gone. Later, my dad sued the ambulance company, which I'd always considered retribution for their incompetence. It was one of the first cases he won. As I stood in the cemetery, I was struck with what it really was: the only way he knew how to grieve.

Peggy's name was on a headstone too, and beneath it a dash with 1935 engraved on one side, and a blank space on the other. I laid a few flowers over each name, not sure whether I should put them above or across the stone, not sure if I should put flowers over the name of a person who wasn't actually dead. I felt suddenly embarrassed at how flimsy they seemed there, limp on the wet grass, where someone could mistake them for something dropped, not placed. I wished I'd bought several more bouquets. I curled my hands back into my sleeves, colder now that I'd stopped moving. I'd never met any of these people, never really mourned them. They had always felt more like the word *ancestor* than anything else. But here, looking down at their names, I thought about their houses, how my breath fogged up their living room windows. My hand cleared out a small circle in the dust. They were right under my soaking feet, while four hundred miles away my grandma was burying herself alive. In a squat, with my calves starting to hurt, with the hood of my rain jacket covering my face, I sobbed for several minutes, to no one in particular.

My grandma had been emailing asking if I'd seen the second house. The most recent email had the subject: YOU SHOULD HAVE LANDED. The body just said: ANY NEWS? I wrote the truest good thing I could think of.

Hey Grandma,

The grass is well cut. The garage paint is peeling a lot, like the city said, but I don't think it'd be too hard to take care of. I did see damage to the roof. I saw some photo albums and a drawer full of papers through the window. Maybe I'll get them sometime.

Storm Lake is nice. The water is really beautiful. I hadn't remembered that part. The neighborhood looks good and green and there's a lot of families and kids playing outside. The drive down was pretty in an Iowa way. It seems like a nice place to live.

Love,

Emily

I wanted to make one last stop and drive by the house where she grew up, the farm with the richest dirt I'd ever touched. It was sold to someone a long time ago, and had since burned down, but I wanted to see the fields roll past my window. It was farther out than the cemetery, and I kept turning onto the wrong dirt roads. Finally, frustrated, I pulled off and called my grandma for directions. When she picked up, I braced myself, expecting her to sound as bad as last night, or even worse. Twenty years ago, the last time I visited this place, she was so ashamed that she wouldn't let me in. Last night, the shame had turned to something like terror. Now, I'd finally seen it all—the house, the town, the other house, the graves. To my surprise, the voice on the other end sounded cheerful. As she spoke, I gave up on the farm and drove back to the main street. I turned into the parking lot of the Dollar Tree and sat in the car listening, for an hour. She started telling me more stories about Storm Lake, wanted to know where we ate lunch, if we said hi to her neighbor, Bob. She was even entertaining the idea of visiting the place herself. When a fear that heavy lifts that fast, you're left to wonder where it went. I'd finally peered into her window, but I'd still chosen not to open the door. Was she relieved that I'd glimpsed how she lived, or that I'd seen only slivers and then turned away? I once thought that by abandoning something, you also abandoned the space it took up in your mind. I thought that, once you stopped seeing it, touching it, you got to stop caring about it, too, like throwing an apple core out the window of a moving car. But it was clear, now, that abandoning something is more like saying it's *dead to you*. The attachment is never really yours to sever.

As we checked out of the Super 8, I noticed a message on the welcome board in the lobby, white felt letters wobbling across a black background.

THE PAST

THE PRESENT

&

THE FUTURE

ARE REALLY ONE

THEY ARE TODAY

ENJOY IT

SEE YA ALONG THE WAY

The house could cave in on its contents, but someone would
still inherit the ruined piles. It all intermingled. Paper tangled in
nests, nests of wings and blankets and cords, cords tangled like
necklaces and unbrushed hair. Supposedly one day it would all
return to dust, but the piles would outlive me while I waited.
Before the dirt swallowed them they'd live alongside it, all the
kinds there were. Living dirt was soil and dead dirt was dirt,
dung dirt and grave dirt, dirt the interstices between types of
life, dirt that swallowed orange rinds and apple cores. Everyone
wastes the core because they think the seeds are poison, but
anything's poison if you have too much of it, even water. The
seeds are poison only if you eat too many. If you just have one
apple, you can eat the core too.

Acknowledgments

Mo Crist is my editor and Clare Mao is my agent, and they both are as patient as they are smart. I feel so lucky to work with them.

I'd also like to thank Melanie Tortoroli and the whole Norton team for helping this book into the world.

My dad gave me enough to fill a book, and for that I thank him. My mom is barely in the book, and for that I thank her. My grandma is an open book. All of them helped raise me, and I really do love them, a lot.

Alyse, Kylie, and Sky read all my drafts and held my hand in malls across the country.

Kerry Howley and Melissa Febos were genius and generous advisors.

Ralph Savarese first showed me what essays could be.

Brittany, Dina, Katie, Lucy, and Micah pruned and soothed my brain in and out of workshop.

Abby, Chris, Jess, Laura, Quinn, and Sylvie are some of my oldest friends and readers.

Babycat, Dot, and Nancy—my exes.